Own a Steel Boat
Mike Pratt

INTERNATIONAL MARINE
PUBLISHING COMPANY
CAMDEN, MAINE 04843

Published in the United States of America
by International Marine Publishing Company, Camden, Maine

Published simultaneously in Great Britain
by Hollis & Carter, an associate company
of The Bodley Head Ltd, London, England

CONTENTS

MEASUREMENTS

In so far as possible, I have used measurements natural to British practice. As there has been a change-over from Imperial to Metric measure in Britain, this means that both types will be quoted throughout the book. A conversion table is supplied below for those who are more used to working in one system than in the other.

M.P.

millimetres	mm. or inches	inches
25·4	1	0·04
50·8	2	0·08
76·2	3	0·12
101·6	4	0·16
127·0	5	0·20
152·4	6	0·24
177·8	7	0·28
203·2	8	0·32
228·6	9	0·35
254·0	10	0·39
508·0	20	0·79
762·0	30	1·18
1016	40	1·58
1270	50	1·97
1524	60	2·36
1778	70	2·76
2032	80	3·15
2286	90	3·54
2540	100	3·94

INTRODUCTION

When we first looked at *Abraxis*, our 44 ft. steel staysail schooner, we knew nothing about steel as a construction material. We had the conventional English prejudice against steel boats and some vague feeling that they must be both prone to rust and difficult to repair. However, *Abraxis* was a boat of the size we wanted for living aboard and for extended voyaging. Better still, she was at a price we could afford and with a reasonable amount of equipment. So we bought her. The fact that she was steel and very rusty gave us horrible qualms, but we had fallen in love with her despite her appearance. The trip down to Penzance to part with the money saw us avidly reading Eric Hiscock's *Sou' West in 'Wanderer IV'* to give us confidence— 'If a steel boat is all right for him, it must be all right for us.'

Three years of fitting out, conversion work, and replating, and three summer voyages that have taken us as far as the Baltic have convinced us that steel is THE material, both for working with and living with. Conversions and repairs are simple and cheap, and when at sea the robust construction gives an immense feeling of confidence. Such is the versatility of steel construction that we have been able to modify drastically the original design to suit our needs exactly, so we are unlikely ever to be looking for a different boat. But were we to do so, she would have to be steel.

All along we have found it difficult to obtain information about steel as a boatbuilding material. Books on the subject are few, and those that do exist seem to be aimed at the professional builder rather than at the owner, and the books tend to be written from the point of view of one builder or one designer. So during holidays I visited yards in Britain, Holland, Belgium and France, to compare ideas and extract the best. This accumulated experience, plus what I have learned through trial and error, is the basis of this book. The book is written from the viewpoint of someone who has to pay the bills, and live with the result of his work.

Most of the experience I have gained has been through trial and error. In many ways this is the most effective way of learning. But it is also expensive. If this book helps to save money and time in this learning process I shall be well pleased. But I hope my writing will also spark off a few new ideas as to how steel boats can be made and mended more cheaply and quickly. In England we have a lot to learn about steel building methods. But interest is escalating. Up until the mid 1970s only a handful of steel boats were available in England. Now scores of yards are building them. And there seems every indication that steel is bringing a revival to the small one-off builder who in former times may have plied his trade in wood. This means more choice for the customer who is sick of the rows of plastic nonentities with which he has been confronted at boat shows for so long. Now he can choose a boat tailored to his needs, rather than one designed for the average family of 3·7. Moreover, his boat will probably be stronger, cheaper and more durable than a GRP version. And there will certainly be a greater pride in ownership. The more so, if the owner has himself taken part in the building.

There are many forms of structure, many methods of construction. Each professional has his own preference. Each system works, and each has its own snags. I do not claim to be an expert, and I am not setting out to prove what methods are best. However, I have been able to see the professional methods from a detached viewpoint. And I have tried to extract those that are likely to be of value to amateurs, bearing in mind amateur-type equipment and facilities. But just as the professionals have their own ideas, so too will amateurs. You sift over, and you extract what appeals, then add your own methods. This is all part of the fun.

My thanks to Paul Stubbs who drew the diagrams, to Dick Everitt, who provided the boat plans, to Jude Watson, who did the typing, and of course to Denny Desoutter, without whose help and encouragement I would never have achieved a long-held ambition to write.

Mike Pratt
Lisbon, 1978

1   A Dutch steel-built tender.

I

Why Steel?

All materials have their problems, but steel has a reputation for having more than most. That this reputation is totally undeserved is something that will be demonstrated during the course of this book.

The adverse talk about steel stems largely from ignorance about the use of the material for small boats in England and America, where there has long been a tradition for the production of wooden boats. When wood no longer lent itself to modern production-line techniques in these countries, glass-reinforced plastic (GRP) took over. Such was not the case in some European countries, in particular Holland and Belgium, where the shortage of trees led to an early switch to iron and then steel production. Steel boats showed themselves to be capable of comparatively rapid production using semi-skilled labour. A tradition of small work-boat and yacht construction in steel thus grew up which has been supplemented but not displaced by GRP. Virtually all work-boats and the majority of yachts in Holland are made of steel. Even little rowing boats and tenders are made of it (photo 1). And they are mostly very smart indeed.

The three main problems that the critics of steel would probably put forward are:

1 Corrosion
2 Condensation
3 Interference with instrumentation

The effects of these problems and how to overcome them will be dealt with in later chapters, but a word of introduction may be useful here.

Corrosion

Rust is not the problem that the potential purchaser of a steel boat may be led to believe. In fact, steel produces a considerable amount of rust for a comparatively small loss of good metal— for example $\frac{1}{16}$ in. plate completely corroded would produce about an inch of rust. What is more, even small amounts of rust can be prevented by a sound paint scheme. More of a problem, though, is electrolysis below the waterline. This is an electro-chemical reaction which can reduce good metal to a non-metallic state in a comparatively short space of time. One particular boat sank on her moorings less than six months after first being launched, directly as a result of electrolysis. You will not need me to tell you that such catastrophes must be extremely rare. That they are so is because electrolytic action can be fairly easily controlled by a sound understanding of the nature of the process and of the several control schemes available.

Condensation

This need not be a problem at all. Experience shows that a well ventilated and insulated steel boat is often less prone to condensation than many wooden boats, and usually less so than a GRP boat. Furthermore, contrary to popular belief, she is usually several degrees cooler below decks in hot weather than her wood or GRP counterpart.

Instrumentation

Steel boats do give rise to certain instrumentation problems, particularly in connection with compass and radio installations. Again, however, the problems are easily overcome by a sound understanding of the magnetic effects of steel and the ways in which these can be counteracted.

These problems are mentioned at the outset, not to put off the would-be owner/builder, but to stress from the beginning that although steel has its vices these are far outweighed by its virtues. The apparent disadvantages of the material can be easily overcome with a basic understanding of its nature.

The Strength of Small Steel Boats

Compared with vessels made out of other materials, steel boats are enormously strong, and small steel boats are relatively stronger than big ones. For example, the hull bottom plating of *Abraxis* is $\frac{1}{4}$ in. thick, the same as that of most barges of ten times the gross tonnage, and large ships are built out of plate of not much greater thickness. The sizes of both the plate and the frames in a small ship will be selected to give a margin for several years' corrosion and to prevent the buckling that can take place with thin plate either in construction or in subsequent contact with quays etc., rather than for strength. The minimum thickness plate I would recommend for any integral part of a small boat would be $\frac{1}{8}$ in., and even this would be recommended for the reasons just stated, there being ample strength in thinner plate for most purposes.

The considerable local strength is testified by a number of incidents. *Abraxis* was driven at hull speed (around eight knots) into one of the Barrow Deep buoys in the Thames Estuary (not with me on watch I hasten to add!) There was a clang Big Ben would have been proud of, but barely a scratch on the port bow where she hit. The average wood or GRP boat would have been stove in. Examples also exist of steel yachts being driven on to coral reefs and pounded there until refloated, the only damage being to the paintwork. Perhaps the best example is provided by David Lewis's gallant little 32 ft. *Ice Bird* (photo 2). Built out of only $\frac{1}{8}$ in. plate, she survived three capsizes in her incredible voyage to Antarctica and back. (See David Lewis, *Ice Bird*, and Chapter 2 of this book.)

Steel's strength is, of course, essential for small work-boats but it is useful for cruising yachts too, enabling them to use commercial harbours with greater confidence and thus

2 David Lewis's *Ice Bird (courtesy of David Lewis)*.

perhaps avoid the expense and similarity of the yacht marinas. At sea, of course, a powerful steel hull induces an enormous feeling of confidence, especially if the ship is split into watertight compartments.

Finally, the high local strength makes for simplicity when it comes to adding deck fittings. Chain plates can be welded on the side and mooring bollards can be welded straight on to the deck. Hatches etc. can be fitted without the structural considerations that would be necessary with other materials.

Complete Watertightness

Comfort aboard a boat is largely linked to how dry the inside can be kept. There is nothing worse than being confronted by drips over your bunk after a cold, wet watch. If water does leak into the boat it is virtually impossible to find anything dry aboard after only a short while at sea. A properly welded steel hull will not leak at all. It is advisable to take full advantage of this property of steel by having decks made of the material as well as the hull. The one disadvantage to this is weight. However, comparatively thin plate can be used ($\frac{1}{8}$ in.), and provided this is allowed for in the design, no problems should arise. In addition to ensuring a dry boat, steel decks will probably be about two-thirds the cost of plywood decks. Not only is steel cheaper than plywood of sufficient thickness, but it does not need expensive fastenings such as stainless bolts. Further, a steel deck may well be completed more quickly than plywood because of the difficulty of securing unlike materials with adequate strength. Those who are able to contemplate a laid deck will not be concerned with cost or speed; nevertheless I would still urge them to lay the wood over steel (techniques for this are described later) because of the gain in strength and watertightness.

Fire Resistance

Of all the materials, steel is the only one that offers real resistance to damage by fire. From personal experience, I know this to be a valuable asset. A serious fire on board *Abraxis* off Cornwall's Lizard Head would have been disastrous had the boat not been steel. Built of wood or GRP she would have been under the waves in minutes, and I guess the crew would have been too, as the liferaft was right above where the outbreak started. As it was, the decks got red hot and the inside was extensively damaged, but we made port in one piece.

Amateur Construction

Steel is well suited to amateur construction because most of the work can be done with basic equipment and the skills required can be picked up in a fairly short time. A round-bilge hull is probably beyond the scope of the average amateur (unless he has access to plate-rolling machinery, which is unlikely). Nevertheless, there are examples of boats of this type being successfully completed. On the other hand, double or triple-chine boats are much easier as very little plate curvature is required, and curves in more than one plane can be avoided. Narrow boats (see p. 38) are easier still to construct.

Working with steel is comparatively rapid, especially in a yard set up for boatbuilding. As a result, labour cost in relation to material cost is lower than with other hull materials. Accordingly, it is worth obtaining quotes for the professional construction of the hull alone. The price may come as a favourable surprise. This avoids the risk of producing a badly finished hull which would probably be worth less than the cost of the steel. Such failures are often to be found for sale, but any money put into their fitting out would be largely wasted, there being little resale value for badly built amateur steel boats. It is the superstructure and the fitting out that take most of the time and it is here that the amateur may well be advised to use his own labour. A useful approximation is that a third of the cost of the boat goes into the hull and the remainder into the fitting out and rigging.

Flush decks have many advantages for amateur construction, it being much easier to lay flat plates on to deck beams than to make complicated coach roofs and dog-houses. It may even make sense, time-wise, to have a slightly bigger boat to avoid the necessity for a coach roof. In any event, slightly higher topsides to accommodate the flush deck should not be a problem for a cruising yacht and will make for a drier boat. If a poop deck can also be included in the design, it is very simple to construct and gives a very useful after cabin.

Costing

It is difficult to compare the comparative costs of various materials because so much depends on the size and type of boat, but in general steel will be cheaper than all other forms of construction, with the possible exception of ferro-cement.

The larger the boat, the greater proportionally will be the saving. Eric Hiscock discovered that in the 50 ft. range, a Dutch-built steel yacht would be roughly two-thirds the cost of its equivalent built in England in wood. (Hence *Wanderer IV* is of steel construction. See Eric Hiscock, *Sou' West in 'Wanderer IV'*, and photo 3.) At the lower end of the scale, a

3   Eric Hiscock's *Wanderer IV (courtesy of Eric Hiscock)*.

production steel hull of around 24 feet will show little saving on a GRP equivalent, although an amateur-built version would undoubtedly be cheaper.

In the following table, I have taken a 40 ft. flush decked cruising yacht hull to be built to a one-off design as an example, in order to compare costs. I have used steel construction as the base of 100. The figures are, of course, only approximate.

Material	Cost-Base 100
Steel	100
Ferro-cement	110
Planked wood	180
Plywood	200
Aluminium	250

GRP hasn't been included because of the difficulty and expense of building one-offs.

The skill of the builder must obviously be taken into account when comparing building times for various materials, but on average the completion time for steel, ferro-cement and plywood should be very similar. Construction in planked wood is a very lengthy process for the amateur, especially as for much of the work two people are needed. Even strip planking is very time-consuming. For example, a 45 ft. William Garden-designed hull recently completed in Lincolnshire took its owner five years to build in strip planked mahogany. Aluminium boats can be constructed rapidly, although considerable skill is required when it comes to the welding. Gas-shielded welding (see Chapter 3) is really necessary and even then, welding of aluminium is nowhere near as simple as it is with steel. Against this, aluminium can be shaped quite easily and can be cut readily with a good electric jig-saw.

Second-hand steel boats are usually cheaper in England or

America than either wood or GRP. This is partly because of steel's poor reputation in some quarters and partly because steel boats are for some reason often less smartly finished than their wood or GRP cousins. This is probably because steel craft owners are often more concerned with the strength and seaworthiness of their boats than with developing an aesthetically pleasing appearance, and with that attitude I have some sympathy. Nevertheless, steel boats can be made to look every bit as attractive as boats made out of any other material. I only need to cite *Minots Light* (photo 4 and see Arthur Beiser, *The Proper Yacht*) as an example.

Steel boats on the second-hand market can, therefore, be an attractive proposition. The fact that a steel boat may appear to be in a dilapidated condition should not necessarily put off the would-be purchaser. Indeed, a bargain may

4 *Minots Light (courtesy of Arthur Beiser).*

be found in this way, as the rust streaks that betray a period of neglect will seldom be serious, although to the uninitiated they may appear disastrous. Nothing could have appeared worse than *Abraxis* when we first found her, but beneath the rust staining there was very sound plating indeed. In any event, some serious plate deterioration is not in itself a reason for rejecting an otherwise satisfactory boat, it is simply a reason for reducing the price. It is seldom that the plating on an entire boat will be poor. Usually metal is wasted in identifiable areas (see Chapter 15 on Corrosion), so all that may be necessary to renew the life of the ship is to replate locally. The procedures for this are described in Chapter 16, but suffice for the moment to say that replating is not difficult. It is considerably easier than building a new boat, and very often slightly suspect steel craft can be purchased for little more than the price of the steel. In addition, the sound steel on older boats will almost certainly be thicker than that of which more modern ones are constructed and possibly of better quality too.

Ease and Cost of Repair

Steel boats are undoubtedly repaired more easily and quickly (and therefore more cheaply) than any other form of construction. The main reason for this is the high local strength of steel, which means that only the area of damage need be removed and new plate welded in. In a wooden boat many planks may have to be replaced as repairs using only short ends are seldom satisfactory and would not be passed by a supervising surveyor. In GRP it may often be impossible to repair the result of serious collision damage satisfactorily because of the monocoque (stressed skin) nature of GRP construction—the strength of any part depends on the strength of the whole. Another factor which influences repairs and costs is availability of materials. Steel is a very commonplace material and can be found virtually anywhere in the world. The same does not apply to good quality wood. In addition, steel in the quantities necessary for the average damage repair is very cheap, such that materials will probably form only a minute part of the repair bill (attractive from the amateur's point of view). Further, quantities of steel adequate for all but major rebuilds can easily be carried aboard as part of the ballast. *Abraxis* carries a selection of angle and round bar together with $\frac{1}{4}$ in., $\frac{3}{16}$ in., $\frac{1}{8}$ in., and some $\frac{1}{16}$ in. plate.

A factor which may well influence yard repair bills is that steel can be worked on immediately and in virtually any weather. No waiting for the area to dry out, as is necessary with wood or GRP, this being especially significant if the repair is below the waterline. This fact will also benefit the amateur who hires a slip on a daily basis to do repairs himself.

Ease of Modification
Another distinct advantage of steel, especially from the point of view of a would-be dream-boat owner is the ease with which existing steel boats can be modified or converted. Our dream-boat seeker, therefore, no longer has to find the perfect boat on the second-hand market; he can find one that is nearly right and modify it to suit his own particular needs. For example, I thought nothing of converting our own after-cockpit schooner into a centre-cockpit version, by cutting away the entire after-deck and dog-house and substituting a poop-deck. An 83 ft. steel schooner built on the Medway to the owner's design was cut in half at the stern and widened to give a more attractive shape to the transom.

Nick Walker, a friend of ours, put a second deck on his old Clyde Puffer *Vic 32* (see Chapter 2) to provide more room for charterers. Such conversions can be done simply, quickly and strongly. Virtually anything can be done with steel, all that is necessary is a little design flair so that the resulting work of art appears that way to other people as well as to you! On the commercial side, many barges and fishing-boats are altered, usually to increase their size to more economic proportions. In Holland barges are often increased in length simply by cutting them in half and adding a new section in the middle.

This versatility provides plenty of scope for the amateur. Many small steel work-boats come on the second-hand market out of trade and all that is needed is the imagination to see the conversion possibilities to use as a pleasure-boat, floating home, or even in a different trade. Quite often small steel craft are uneconomic for their large company owners but may be made to earn a living for an owner/skipper.

Comparison of Hull Materials

To make a comparison of hull building materials is not altogether useful as so much depends on personal taste. Nevertheless the various materials available do have certain specific advantages and disadvantages which are worth pointing out.

Planked Wood

ADVANTAGES Aesthetic appeal. Repairs can be done (given time) using simple hand tools. Damaged paintwork can be left for a considerable period without detriment to the ship's fabric.

DISADVANTAGES Subject to attack by marine borers (teredo, gribble, etc.). Prone to leaks. Poor local strength. Seams tend to open up in warm climates.

Strip Planked Wood

ADVANTAGES Relatively simple form of construction, avoiding the necessity for extensive framing. Greater watertightness than with conventional planked construction.

DISADVANTAGES   As with conventional wood construction but additionally the wood is prone to stress cracking with changes in climatic conditions (difficult to prevent and almost impossible to repair). Repairs are difficult and expensive as this form of construction relies on its monocoque nature for its strength.

Plywood

ADVANTAGES   Simplicity and speed of construction. Cold moulding techniques can provide good total strength. Impervious to marine borers (they cannot get through the glue).

DISADVANTAGES   Designs limited to chined construction often giving a boxlike appearance (unless expensive cold moulding techniques are used). Danger of delamination (break-up of the glue joints in the plywood laminations). Low second-hand value of plywood boats, normally because of their fairly limited life potential.

GRP

ADVANTAGES   Comparative simplicity of maintenance (freedom from maintenance is a myth, no boat is free from maintenance). Total watertightness. Production-line techniques can be used which can make the product cheaper.

DISADVANTAGES   Lack of aesthetic appeal. Condensation (especially in cheaper boats with poor ventilation and insulation). Low local strength, unless abnormally heavy laminations are used. Difficulty of satisfactory repair to structural damage. Difficulty of building one-offs or undertaking modifications.

Aluminium

ADVANTAGES Very light and very strong. Can last extremely well unprotected by paint.

DISADVANTAGES Extremely expensive. Difficult to obtain in small quantities and specific sizes necessary for ship-building. Can corrode extremely rapidly if suitable precautions against electrolysis are not taken and maintained. Specialist gear really needed for welding, though cutting is simpler than with steel.

In my opinion aluminium is not suitable for use by the amateur, although I say this mindful of the fact that *Trigillis*, the most professional-looking boat I have ever seen built outside a yard, was made of the material.

Ferro-cement

ADVANTAGES Suitability for amateur construction on the cheap, being labour-not-material-intensive. Lends itself to the production of one-offs with no limit to the designs that can be (and have been!) produced. Freedom to adopt curved shapes. Reasonable local and total strength and watertightness.

DISADVANTAGES Weight; especially in smaller boats. Plastering is critical; mistakes made at this stage are difficult to rectify. Prone to stress cracking and flaking; particularly true in tropical climates. Difficulty in assessing the condition of second-hand ferro boats, which can lead to a low second-hand value.

The above comments are not exhaustive, they simply identify the main pros and cons.

Conclusion

I certainly would not contend that steel is THE perfect material for all situations. A potential owner must assess its merits and its problems in relation to his own criteria, one of which will probably be the aesthetic appeal of the material itself. For many tasks steel will be the most suitable material, for some it may not be appropriate at all.

2

What Can be Done

Build or Buy

Whether to buy second-hand or build new must depend on whatever stirs your enthusiasm. On time and financial criteria alone, buying a dilapidated craft and mending or modifying as necessary will usually be the winner. But this may not give the most satisfaction. It is a very positive feeling to look at your newly completed craft and to know that you created her from basic materials.

In this chapter, I offer some examples of what people have done with small steel boats. Building, renovating, modifying and straightforward buying are all included—not so that the reader will necessarily follow in the footsteps of these pages, but simply so that he may have some idea of what can be done.

Steelaway

Tony Porter's choice of name for the 32 ft. steel sloop he made was so apt for both the boat and his own intentions that it came as a big disappointment when a registered *Stealaway* came into our home port, built in of all things, Glass Reinforced Plastic. Still, Tony's is a super boat and all credit is due to him (and Jude) for completing the boat from scratch in what must be a record: little more than one year of part-time work. We nicknamed her *The Tardis* because of the uncanny way she seemed to grow beyond her 32 feet when you were inside, and the way more and more people could be packed in without feeling cramped.

Tony's philosophy was simple: he wanted a strong boat to

5 Tony Porter on *Steelaway*.

sail off to the sun with, he wanted her quickly, and she had to be cheap. Steel was clearly the answer to all these requirements, so Tony set about finding a yard to build him only the simple chined hull, the rest he would do himself. He was fortunate in finding a small yard, who would not only build the hull, but would also let him help in the work, both to learn and to cut down on costs. The hull was completed in record time for under £1,000 (in 1973) and the fitting out began. Tony has a philosophy that anything can be done with a Black and Decker jigsaw (and I am sure from experience that he is not far wrong) so the decks and interior furniture were created at lightning speed with little more than that instrument and a screwdriver. Fittings were bought at minimum cost from hardware shops and the like, chandleries only being used as a last resort. For example, rigging screws were obtained in this manner, showing a considerable saving, even on the comparatively cheap and well-stocked local chandlery. The mast was created from a telegraph pole (bought straight from the importers before it was creosoted)

27

and all the rigging was handspliced by Tony himself.

Steelaway is of simple design as indeed steel boats should be in order to gain full advantage of the material. Chine construction was used so that no expensive plate-rolling machinery was necessary to produce the hull. The first chine was just underwater so that it was not offensive to the eye. Quarter-inch plate was used for the bottom chine plates and for the box-section keel, so that little extra ballast was necessary. Above the water line $\frac{3}{16}$ in. plating was used and this thickness of plating combined with the strength of chine construction (given by the plates meeting at an angle) allowed for virtually frameless monocoque construction, only two main box-section frames being used. The advantages of this form of construction are considerable in terms of weight-, time- and cost-saving, as well as doing away with the angular water (and therefore rust) traps which framed construction creates. The only difficulty is that of obtaining a regular shape to the hull, this being much easier if you can set up the framing first.

What made *Steelaway* somewhat unattractive on first sight was her excessive tumblehome from the gunwale to the flush deck. This also had the disadvantage of producing a small working deck area. I think that were Tony to build the same size of boat again he would go for the higher freeboard and reduced tumblehome, thereby overcoming the above disadvantages and additionally gaining even greater space below.

Abraxis

Our own boat is a good example of the type of post-war, Low Countries built, steel yacht that can often be bought at a reasonable price provided a slightly tatty condition is acceptable. We know very little of her history, except that she was built in Antwerp in 1948 and given the name *Stern*. We know nothing of her doings until 1969 save snippets to the effect that she had been seen in both the Mediterranean and

6 *Abraxis* on the slip for a grit blast and repaint.

Caribbean, and a rumour (probably false) that she had been engaged in gun-running. An American army officer became the owner in 1968 and lavished new things upon the boat including an engine, a 240-volt generator and a new rig. Her present name apparently also stems from this time. Unfortunately, the owner must have overspent, for on reaching Penzance in England from Cork in Southern Ireland the boat suffered the ignominy of a writ being pinned to the mast. And for the next three or four years she lay virtually derelict, grinding up and down the quay in Penzance's coal harbour with scant attention paid to her. That was where we found her in 1974.

Built of $\frac{3}{16}$ in. plate, *Abraxis* is 40 feet long on deck and 32 feet 6 inches on the waterline, with a 10 ft. beam. She has a long straight keel and is similar in hull shape to the Van de

29

Wieles' *Omoo* (also built in Antwerp in about 1948 and subsequently sailed around the world in just over two years—see A. Van de Wiele, *The West in my Eyes*). She has been our home and the subject of most of our spare-time work for the last three years. Her steel construction has enabled us considerably to modify her original design to take account of our own needs. The major modification was that of cutting off the deck and dog-house abaft the after watertight bulk-head and turning this area into a fine, airy after cabin with an inside steering position, navigation area and U-shaped seat-ing. The conversion almost doubled the effective size of the boat and made a very much more spacious home as well as giving considerable advantages at sea.

Avalon

Avalon was professionally built as a yacht in 1955 by the little yard of J. W. Valentijn & Zonen, Langeraar, Holland. She finds her place here because I know her to be an excellent little steel boat built in the true tradition of the small Dutch yards. She is similar in appearance to thousands of boats that appear all over Holland but in my opinion she is one of the best of the designs. M. F. Gunning drew up the plans based on a prototype—*Alcyone*—which was built to meet the following requirements:

1 To serve as a comfortable floating home for his wife and himself for at least two months each year.
2 To have, in addition, plenty of room for two to four guests.
3 To be suitable for Dutch waters, both for the shallow lakes and for the short and vicious seas of the Ijsselmeer, and the higher but longer waves of the estuaries.
4 To be capable of handling by himself with an occasional semi-trained hand at the helm to help out in tight places.

7 *Avalon (courtesy of Denny Desoutter).*

5 To be built—and subject to maintenance—within a strictly limited budget.

6 And last, but not least, to sail well.

Avalon, although only 36 feet long, has an incredible amount of room and gives the impression of spaciousness, sleeping four in two separate cabins and a further two in the saloon where the dinette converts into a fine double bunk. She has been the full-time home of the present owner, Toby Wool-

31

rych—and of the previous owners for a total of around ten years. I quote what the present owner has to say of her:

'She far exceeds the limited seaworthiness conditions laid down. Her twin, *Spurning*, has been around the world, and others have sailed to America, Greece, Scandinavia and Australia. For ease of handling it is difficult to find another boat of similar size which is her peer. She can be sailed with ease single-handed, requiring another crew member to help only when shortening sail or entering or leaving a crowded berth. She is simplicity itself to maintain, requiring only a short, intensive annual repainting/revarnishing exercise of about two weeks' duration to eliminate surface rust and cheer up the woodwork.'

A boat similar to *Avalon* would undoubtedly be an excellent buy for anyone wanting a strong family cruising boat or a voyaging home, but a good second-hand one will be expensive. However, this should not deter the enthusiastic amateur builder, as a steel hull of this configuration could be built comparatively easily and very cheaply. With its flat bottom, chine construction and flush decks it lends itself to steel (more details are given of this type of construction in Chapter 5).

Ice Bird (See photo 2, p. 14)
Whether boat or man turned out to be tougher on David Lewis's famous voyage to Antarctica in 1972–74 is debatable, but what is certain is that steel boats and men of steel make an impressive combination. For those who are not familiar with Dr Lewis's incredible achievement, he set sail alone from Sydney on 19th October, 1972, headed for Antarctica, a voyage never before attempted by a single-handed yachtsman. Fourteen weeks later *Ice Bird* reached a US Antarctic station after surviving 'mountainous seas, constant gales, snow storms, freezing temperatures—and two

capsizes which left her dismasted,' (to quote from introductory remarks to Fontana's paperback edition of David Lewis's *Ice Bird*). On the return leg through pack-ice and towering icebergs the boat again capsized while struggling with weather as atrocious as that endured on the outward passage. Eventually the safety of Cape Town was reached with the boat battered but still intact.

The amazing thing is that *Ice Bird* was not specially designed for the job, as one might imagine, but is a chine boat of very straightforward construction built out of comparatively thin $\frac{1}{8}$ in. plate. Her length overall is 32 feet, the beam is 9 feet 6 inches and the draft 6 feet, so she is by no means a big boat. The only strengthening that was done to the fabric of the vessel to enable her to undertake the voyage was in connection with the rudder, cabin windows and washboards. An extension was welded on from the keel to give further support to the rudder, $\frac{1}{8}$ in. plate was bolted over the windows to prevent them stoving in in heavy weather, and the lower washboards were replaced by steel welded in place. In other respects she was a fairly typical production boat. Indeed, Lewis's search for a suitable vessel that led him to *Ice Bird* took him only a little more than a week.

An obvious lesson to draw from this is that a small steel boat can go absolutely anyplace where there is water if handled by the right crew. What is relevant here, though, is that vessels of this type of construction can be obtained fairly cheaply, and they are readily available especially in Holland. Better still, the simplicity of construction renders building from scratch well within the capabilities of the skilled amateur.

Xylonite

Steel boats just out of trade often fetch very little; seldom more and often less than the scrap value of the steel together with the second-hand value of any machinery sold along with

33

them. Such was the case with *Xylonite*, an ex-sailing barge of 110 tons burden who had served out her days after the age of sail as a motor barge on the London river. Her plating was in excellent condition when Tim Elliff bought her, as was her recently overhauled Gardner 6LW power unit. She was in every respect a vessel worth restoring to her former glory and this was exactly what Tim set out to do. No structural repairs were necessary whatsoever, so work could be started straight away on the major projects of re-rigging and fitting out the inside as a floating home with charter accommodation.

In the necessary work, the fact that *Xylonite* was steel was of considerable advantage. Chain plates, crab winches and other fittings could be simply and speedily welded on. Steel spars were chosen because of their strength (and availability at the right price) and the mast case for the main mast was a simple fabrication job welded straight to the deck. Not that I am trying in any way to under-estimate Tim's achievement in getting the boat, just out of trade, into racing trim in under six months; but this illustrates how steel construction in any size of vessel can save time and money. And Tim praises the steel decks for the absence of drips, especially after owning a wooden barge.

Before the reader chases out to buy a steel Thames barge, I must confess that there are only a few of them left now. However, they can still be found. For those who don't set store by owning a traditional Thames barge, several alternatives present themselves. Lighters can be purchased very cheaply in good condition on the London river. Small ones used to be virtually given away because they were uneconomic, but now the new-found interest in the annual barge rowing race has meant an increase in demand for these craft. Even so, little ones can be had for not much more than scrap value and some bigger lighters have gone for less. Meat lighters are best, because they have a complete wooden lining inside the steel. This only has to be cleaned (sand blasting is easiest and cheapest in the long run) and sealed to give a very presentable interior which needs a bit of furniture to make very homely. Lighters, of course, have no means of propulsion and no means of steerage, so without anything being done in this direction they are only suitable as immobile houseboats. However, rudders are easy enough to make out of steel or may even be purchased complete. And stern gear is easy to fit in a steel vessel (see Chapter 14). Engine installation should normally be simple, as mounting brackets can be welded in position on the basis of a cardboard model of the engine (see Chapter 14), and the engine can be slotted in with no strengthening required. In addition to mechanized propulsion, swim-headed lighters have been converted to sail, rigged spritsail fashion (e.g. *Montreal*).

If a mobile barge just out of trade is required, why not look to Holland where many fine smaller motor barges are being laid up because of their uneconomic size.

8 A Dutch motor barge, converted to houseboat.

Moving to slightly smaller commercial craft, ex-fishing-boats can make excellent pleasure craft and mobile homes, or perhaps the skipper/owner may be able to make a success of one commercially. Fishing-boats in England of around the 40 ft. mark are usually wooden, but steel ones do find their way on to the market (often originating in Holland or Belgium).

Good fishing-boats can be bought comparatively cheaply in England (fishing is not very profitable for the small man), depending on the state of the power unit and on the gear that is being sold with the boat.

Sometimes special circumstances apply. For example, a while back bigger fishing-boats were going more cheaply because of particularly onerous legislation by the British government concerning fishing vessels of over 45 feet. An expensive survey was required together with totally uneconomic modifications. Many vessels were being shortened in any way possible, to get them under 45 feet (easy with steel, not so easy with wood). But around the 50 ft. size it was difficult to do much reduction, so these boats had to be sold off cheaply.

Vic 32

What an incredible enthusiast's boat *Vic 32* is—an old Clyde Puffer, she was built in 1943 to carry 150 tons of cargo on the

9   The old Clyde puffer, *Vic 32*.

River Clyde and the west coast of Scotland. She was, and still is, propelled by steam. Her main boiler is huge, about 20 feet high, and her engine room is a joy to behold, with its huge polished brass pressure dials and massive crankshaft (which you lubricate by simply squirting oil on to the big end journals) it's a delight to anyone who appreciates the beauty of steam. Best, though, is when the engine is running. Almost complete silence prevails with just a slight hiss of escaping steam and a swish as the shaft turns—but what incredible power as she glides silently away from a quay! What a contrast to the modern ship's engine room where no communication is possible over the noise of the diesels, and where all romance is gone!

When Nick Walker (the present owner) bought *Vic* she had been lying derelict in Whitby for so long that her hold had come to be used as the local rubbish tip. All manner of junk had to be disposed of before work could commence on the seized-solid steam engines. Still, she was cheap, approximately scrap value which was little more than £1,000. Weekend after patient weekend gradually brought the day nearer when the boiler could be fired up. This was a critical time, as the boiler is the vulnerable part of a steam engine, the engine itself being so chunky that hammers and blowlamps can be applied to get the thing to turn. By contrast any damage to the boiler, especially to the boiler tubes, is not only extremely difficult and expensive to repair, but also very dangerous owing to the high pressure which is built up inside. But the boiler was fired, it didn't explode and eventually the way was clear for the voyage to London. This was achieved without incident and the conversion work necessary for chartering back in her home waters was started.

One of the major tasks was the doubling of available space by splitting the hold into two decks. This was done simply and quickly because of the steel construction, and masses of charter space was gained, and what a splendid home she will make! The other major task was to attend to the steelwork of the hull. She is an old boat and had suffered her fair share of corrosion, but this was not too much of a problem with steel. I shudder to think about the task of repairing the equivalent rot in a wooden boat. Nick first of all sand-blasted the hull to see the extent of the problem. And as is usually the case, the corrosion turned out to be not as bad as anticipated, with the worst problem on the waterline.

The solution was not difficult—simply weld doubling plates all around the boat covering the waterline, and the boat would last many a year. These were flat plates, so no rolling was required and the job was done in a fortnight.

I give this boat as an example, not necessarily to fire people with enthusiasm for Puffers, but as an illustration of the diverse opportunities that exist for buying and converting steel boats out of trade. Nick's previous boat was yet another example. A steel narrow boat of some 80 feet, she was based at Brentford on the English canal system where she made an excellent home and pleasure cruiser.

Narrow Boats

Narrow boats tend to vary only in length as their breadth is determined by the width of the canals through which they are designed to travel. Thus it is that this form of craft can almost literally be built by the mile and just cut off to length as

10 A narrow boat, for rambling in rural England.

required. They must be the simplest boats in the world to make, having flat bottoms and flat sides and almost flat ends. And yet they can provide an enormous amount of pleasure, enabling one to discover rural England (and parts that are not so rural) at a pace that permits appreciation. The pastime of narrow-boating has recently gained enormous popularity in England, and commercial interests have not failed to notice this. As a result, a narrow boat of the most simple kind, fitted to a rudimentary standard and supplied with a small diesel engine will still be expensive. She could be built by an amateur for a cost of less than a third of the finished price.

Here is an attractive financial proposition for the amateur as well as an interesting project. A boat could be completed in a relatively short period with every hope of doubling one's investment if it is subsequently sold. Alternatively, she might be used as a hire cruiser, reserving a period for one's own holiday. Narrow boats can be placed with hire companies who will charter the vessel out, look after all the paper work and put right all the faults, often of the charterers' making, that appear in the boat. In return, the company will expect a substantial chunk of the profits. They will probably earn it, so you should only consider chartering out directly if you are prepared to turn out at all hours of the day or night to sort out an engine that won't start (probably out of fuel) or a boat that is stuck in the bank. The normal return on a boat bought at retail price is about the commercial rate of interest, but capital appreciation can, of course, also be expected, and this has been relatively high on boats in recent years. If the boat is built for a material cost alone, then the return on investment will be very good.

Make some enquiries about the current situation before jumping into such a project, as economic circumstances change all the time. However, it is worth consideration, and anyone who can weld should be capable of completing the venture satisfactorily.

11 A typical Dutch cabin cruiser.

Cabin Cruisers

A steel cabin cruiser can be cheap to buy and easy to build.
Here is one which is typical of the sort seen all over Holland.

Conclusion

In this chapter, I have tried to give some varied ideas of what
can be done with steel as a material for boat construction.
The examples were chosen so as to give a broad spectrum of
possibilities in the hope that one or more of them may spark
off a thought in the mind of the reader.

3

Tools that will be needed

Contrary to what might be imagined, the specialist tools that will be needed are probably less than those necessary for use with other construction materials. The basic requirements are contained in the following list. Each of the items is examined in more detail later in the chapter.

Arc-welder—plus leads, electrode holder and earth clamp
Angle-grinder—plus a selection of cutting and grinding discs
Masks—a hand-held and helmet version would be useful, plus plenty of spare glasses
Goggles—shaded glass for cutting, clear for grinding and chipping
Leather gloves
Chipping hammer
Cold chisel
Wire brush
Clamps
Engineer's rule and retractable metal tape
Steel set-square
French chalk
File

Gas cutting gear would also be useful, but is not essential. Electrodes are a consumable item and not really a tool, but a brief discussion of them is included later on in the chapter.

Arc-welder
This is an obvious must and will probably be the most

expensive purchase in the above list. Very many different types are available and it is difficult to decide just which one to buy although certain necessary features can be identified. Most important is to ensure that the welder has sufficient capacity for the work that is to be undertaken. Don't make the mistake of buying one that is too small, especially as slightly higher capacity does not usually add significantly to the bill.

The amateur will be best suited with a welder that can be used off ordinary domestic electric supply. With most very powerful machines a higher input voltage will be required, but these are not of much concern to us. What is of concern is the output rating of the welder which will be measured in amps, the higher the amperage the thicker the plate that can be welded. The thickest plate that is normally met with in small-boat construction is 10 mm. (0·39 in.) and this can be easily welded with equipment of 140-amp output. Thicker plate can be welded with a machine of this capacity provided the edges are bevelled and several runs are made. Even though you may not envisage welding thicker than 4 mm., which only requires 110-amp output, a job will certainly arrive sooner or later that will require more. Above 140 amps it is not possible to run from standard 13/15-amp input, so a special supply will normally be the most appropriate.

Some better quality equipments (such as the Oxford range) are capable of varying the input voltage. While the normal UK supply is 240-volt, certain conditions (such as a very long lead from the supply point) can cause a voltage drop which will have a significant effect on performance.

It may well be necessary to consider equipment with this facility if such circumstances apply. Safest is to test the voltage at the likely place of work using an Avo Meter. A small fall below the required voltage will not be significant, but ± 10 per cent or more could be. On one particular job where a long lead to the shore had to be used and several people were drawing off the same socket, my welder would hardly produce a sparkle and we found that the voltage was well below 200. Oxford arc equipment also in use at the same time was persuaded to perform by fitting the input lead onto a lower voltage terminal.

The next decision to be made is whether to go for an *oil-cooled* or an *air-cooled* set. An oil-cooled model has the distinct advantage that it will run for almost any length of time at full capacity without overheating. Consequently it will normally have a very long working life. Many such sets last for ten or twenty years with little attention. Against this, however, must be balanced a number of disadvantages. An oil-cooled set will be considerably heavier than its air-cooled counterpart of similar capability. A 140 amp air-cooled set can be easily carried a considerable distance by one person and is very easy to manoeuvre to different parts of a boat. Such is not the case with an oil-cooled set which will normally require lifting tackle or several people. A lot of shipborne work is in awkward positions to say the least, and a welder that can't be properly sited can add considerably to the length of the job. Weight will also be significant if the equipment is to be carried aboard the boat. An oil-cooled set would make ideal ballast, but the problem is you can hardly put it in the bilge! And another problem is that if the boat heels significantly the oil can slosh out through the air vents of the welder stowed down below.

An air-cooled welder is normally about half the cost of an oil-cooled version, but their relative lives have to be weighed against initial cost. There are a number of cheap poor quality air-cooled sets on the market which will have very limited lives. My first one lasted only six months! On the other hand, many excellent sets are available at only marginally extra cost. Whatever you may buy, it is most important to ensure that the model selected has some sort of thermal cut-out so that it automatically switches itself off before it reaches

43

danger temperature. In winter my own welder will run for several hours of almost continuous welding at maximum output before it reaches cut-out temperature. In hot weather, about one hour is the maximum, and it then requires about ten minutes to cool down. (It is a 'Monowelder', Italian made, obtainable from S.I.P. (Industrial Products) Ltd.) If more than one person is capable of welding so that the set tends to be in continuous use, it can be a problem. However, when I am working on a job by myself, in hot weather, an hour's continuous welding is all I can take without a rest, so the fact that the equipment needs a break as well doesn't matter. Incidentally, my air-cooled set has lasted five years and shows every sign of carrying on for ever. It gets very rough treatment such as being sat in the mud (not to be recommended—but the tide was coming in) while I welded some anode studs on. It has also been hauled up the mast to do a job there. . . . It was even doused by a wave while I was standing in a barge boat trying to weld back a Thames sailing barge's rudder that had come adrift from its mountings. It withstood all such trials with no apparent disadvantage and it is worth saying here that this sort of versatility is just not obtainable from an oil-cooled set. I attribute the good service I get from my set to its thermal cut-out and extremely robust windings and internal connections (I had the top off to look before I bought it).

With air-cooled equipment it is quite often possible to obtain infinitely variable control over amperage setting throughout the output range (choke control). This is normally achieved by a control knob which is turned clockwise or anti-clockwise to increase or decrease the setting. Such a facility is to be recommended as the welder can be precisely geared to the conditions of the job. After a while it is possible to fine tune the control by instinct without reference to the amperage scale, simply by reference to the arc.

Oil-cooled or air-cooled is the decision you will have to

make depending on the type of work to be done. If it is to be general maintenance, and especially if the equipment is to be carried on board, then it must be air-cooled. If a lot of continuous welding is involved from a position where the machine can be sited so that all parts of the job can be reached, then oil-cooled is probably the answer. Welding equipment holds its value fairly well so the oil-cooled set could always be swopped over later when the major construction work is done.

A word about power supply. Even with the sets I have been describing, it is best to obtain 30-amp *input* supply such as would be used for a domestic electric cooker. This is because a 90-amp output welder will take right up to the limit of an ordinary 13-amp input, and sudden overloading such as sticking an electrode, will cause the circuit to fuse. Thirty-amp input is best, but 20 amps would do. The maximum input required can usually be obtained from the welder instruction manual and will commonly be expressed in k.V.A (= 1,000 volt/amperes × a power factor of 0·8). The maximum input required for my 140-amp 'Monowelder' is 4·2 k.V.A. so at 240 volts the following input amperage is necessary:

$$V \times A \times 0\cdot8 = k.V.A.$$
$$240 \times A \times 0\cdot8 = 4,200$$
$$A = 22$$

Input wires themselves should be heavy duty and flexible. If a long run of cable is necessary to the supply point it is best if a single continuous cable is used. Plug and socket connections can cause a sizeable voltage drop and are in any event a weak point in the line where moisture could enter and short out the installation. If a cable has to be joined, the wires should be soldered and taped thoroughly, but even this will cause a weak point as the wires will no longer be flexible. If plugs are used in the input line I would avoid fuses except at the supply point, or a check will have to be made on every fuse if a short occurs. In any event, 13-amp fuses are easily blown by an overload on a 140-amp welder.

At the *output* end the leads supplied with a welder or as an 'extra' are seldom long enough. Six feet is often all that is supplied whereas double that would be useful. Provided long leads are of good quality, thick cable, little power loss will occur at the electrode. But make sure that all connections are clean and tight. Earth clamps can be of two types—either sprung or with a screw thread. The spring type is quicker to move from job to job but the jaws are often too narrow to fit on the work, so that they have to be tack-welded on. Also, they have the habit of springing off. A better earth is obtainable with a threaded clamp and this is the type I would go for. Most electrode holders are spring-loaded and the main point to note is to avoid ones that are too heavy. Hours of continuous welding can put quite a strain on arm and wrist and a little weight saved in the holder can make quite a difference.

Arc-welders are relatively safe pieces of equipment, although that does not mean that they can be treated casually. The danger lies with the 240-volt input supply, which can, of course, be lethal. At the output end there is little danger and it is possible to touch both leads without harm, (although this practice should be avoided because there may be a fault in the machine). The leads have high amperage at comparatively low volts and it is high voltage that is dangerous.

Watching the arc with the naked eye for even a very short time causes arc-eye which is not unlike having sand around the eyeballs. Arc-eye is thoroughly uncomfortable and extremely dangerous and anyone who has experienced it will do all he can to avoid a repetition. To those who have not, I can only say take every precaution against the danger, which means always using a *mask* with darkened glass that is free from cracks. The temptation to peep around the corner of the mask to see a bit better must be resisted, and on no account should gas cutting goggles be used as these will not give sufficient protection.

Electrodes

Many makes of electrode are available for all different materials, so it is up to an individual user to experiment with different rods and find those which suit him best. To express a personal opinion, I do not like British Oxygen's Vodex rods as they seem to me to be designed for much more powerful machines than mine. I have found the Swedish Oerlikon rods, made in Northern Ireland, to be very easy to use and would recommend that anyone who is beginning should start with these.

Whatever rods you use, it is essential that they be stored in a dry place as dampness will quickly destroy their performance. If they do get damp try putting them in the oven for a while before use to dry them out. (The use of various gauges of rod is discussed in Chapter 4.)

In addition to buying ordinary mild steel rods, it may also be useful to obtain some gouging rods. These are specially designed for cutting plate using the arc of the welder. They are harder than ordinary rods and do not have a flux covering. After heating up the plate with the arc from one of these rods using a very high amperage, cutting is achieved by pushing the rod through the plate and moving it along. By repeating this process quite accurate cuts can be made relatively quickly on thin plate. Ordinary mild steel rods can be used for this purpose but they are very quickly expended.

Gas-shielded Welding

Most metals when molten tend to form oxides from the air, and these oxides inhibit the proper flow of metal at the weld. A satisfactory weld is accordingly difficult, if not impossible, to achieve without shielding. This is the main function of flux on electrodes, but an alternative is to use an inert gas to shield the weld. This can be more effective than flux when stainless and certain high-tensile steels are to be welded.

In this technique a gun is used to feed copper-clad electrodes continuously into the weld area through the gas shield. Argon is best used for stainless but a cheaper gas such as carbon dioxide will normally do for high-tensile steel. Advantages are several. A slag-free weld is produced, therefore, saving chipping time between welds, and preventing the possibility of a slag trap and consequent weakness. Another benefit is the time saved through not having to change the electrode. This type of welding inputs far less heat, with consequent minimization of distortion. Although, if too much advantage is taken of the continuous feed, distortion will result through long runs. The cost of the continuous-feed electrode is less, although the gas, especially Argon, can be expensive.

Argon arc-welding is very easy, far easier than stick welding. But the initial cost of the equipment is high—more than ten times that of conventional arc. So it isn't really worth buying unless you are setting up professionally. This is especially true as stick equipment will really be needed as well, because the heavy, cumbersome Argon arc plant isn't easily movable from job to job.

Angle-grinder

The angle-grinder is an essential tool for many tasks. Its principal use will be in smoothing off the cut edges of plate and bevelling them prior to welding. It will also be necessary to grind flush the welded seams. With a sanding disc attached it can be used for cleaning plate of mill-scale and rust before painting. Many ancillary applications will be found, such as sharpening tools and engineering-type fabrications. Perhaps most important of all is the fact that the angle-grinder can be made to cut quite thick plate, fairly rapidly. I have used it on 10 mm. plate successfully and 3 mm. it cuts like butter. On thin plate such as this my grinder is nearly as quick as gas cutting gear and the finished edge is fine for welding without further preparation (unless a bevel is considered necessary). Cutting-discs will definitely be far more expensive than gas, so use the grinder only if small amounts of work are involved or if gas is not available. One 9 in. cutting disc will last roughly 12 feet on 3 mm. plate. Cutting by disc does have the advantage of being much cleaner than gas, which may be useful in some circumstances.

Several makes of angle-grinder are available and all the brand makes will be adequate for our purpose. I would express a personal preference for Wolf, but I had excellent service for five years from my very old, metal-bodied Black and Decker which I bought second-hand for £10. It finally sparked its last only when it was borrowed unbeknown to me to cut through 2 in. ferro-cement.

Some points are worth noting. An all-plastic-bodied version is the safest, as this provides double insulation against shocks caused by faulty wiring. Most of the manufacturers produce their grinders in two forms—an angle-grinder proper, and what is usually described as a power-sander. The difference is normally in the power of the electric motor and sometimes in the robustness of the gearbox. An angle-grinder will normally revolve at upwards of 6,000 r.p.m. whereas the power-sander will work at about 4,500 r.p.m. The grinder will naturally be slightly heavier. There is not usually a significant difference in the price of the two types so I would recommend buying the heavier duty version, especially if cutting is envisaged.

Some manufacturers such as Black and Decker and Wolf produce a mini version known as a 'grinderette'. This can be held in one hand if necessary and may be useful for light jobs, but at about two-thirds the price of the grown-up version there seems little point in buying one.

Angle-grinders can be extremely dangerous tools so certain basic factors must always be observed:

1 Always wear goggles. They may steam up, they may be uncomfortable and you may see better without them, but the pain of a metal splinter in your eye is something you will never forget. I have had it twice through sheer stupidity—I have used each of the above excuses. Both times I was lucky and no permanent damage was done, just a week or more of discomfort. There won't be a next time because I might not be so lucky then. Loick Fougeron lost his eye because he was not able to get a metal sliver removed as he was on his boat some way from civilization.

2 Make sure the machine is turned off before connecting to the mains. The immense torque when starting can cause the grinder to spin a considerable distance, doing damage to people, property or itself. Again I know through personal experience!

3 The grinder can easily be spun out of your hands by the starting torque so it must be held very securely and care should be taken not to lose balance.

4 Be careful to avoid cutting through the wire with the disc. The results are dramatic!

5 The work should be securely clamped to a bench or something solid to avoid the possibility of it shooting off and injuring someone or twisting a cutting disc thereby causing it to fracture. The projectiles caused by a fractured disc can be lethal.

6 Always use the guard which will be supplied with the machine. (Power-sanders won't have one.) This will deflect fractured disc or metal splinters away from you, but, more important, will protect your hands and arms should you slip.

7 Cutting with an angle-grinder can be quite dangerous, so be very careful especially while the 'knack' is being acquired. The disc tends to spin out of the groove that is being cut and to shoot anywhere. This must be resisted by holding the disc down into the groove and cutting with the leading edge. It is additionally important to maintain a stable stance.

8 The stream of glowing red-hot particles that the grinder emits can do a lot of damage, and they can carry a considerable distance. Glass-fibre boats in particular are susceptible and the sparks can easily catch clothing alight if attention is paid to the job without watching where the stream of molten metal is going. I once managed to set my shoe alight in this way!

Protective Clothing

Goggles have already been mentioned above in the context of the use of the angle-grinder, but they will also be needed for chipping slag or rust. The second splinter I imbedded in one of my eyes was caused by chipping rusty metal above head level. Goggles are cheap enough to have several pairs so you can throw them away as soon as they become scratched and difficult to see through. That is when the temptation can arise to do without them in order to see better. One point to remember when buying goggles is to avoid those that have excessively large holes in the side for ventilation. I have known splinters to get through these and to do nasty injuries. You need clear ones for grinding and chipping and coloured ones for gas cutting. Goggles are available which combine clear and coloured, with the latter on a fold-back hinge.

Shields will be required for use with the arc-welder, both to protect the eyes from the bright light of the arc and the face from spitting metal. The shield will have a view panel in the centre consisting of darkened glass sandwiched between clear. The darkened glass is protected by the clear which can be thrown away as soon as weld splatter begins to hinder vision. If the darkened glass becomes cracked, it should be rejected immediately as the eyes can be damaged by rays through the crack without any danger being apparent. Shields come in two forms: either a hand-held mask or a helmet which fits on your head and is hinged so that you push it back when not needed. Which to use is a matter of personal choice. A helmet has definite advantages as it leaves both hands free. Nevertheless I have never been able to get on with them, so I always use the hand-held mask. I never seem to be able to adjust my helmet properly and it has the habit of dropping an inch at a crucial moment. Plus there is the danger with the helmet of welding your free hand to the job!

Always wear *leather gloves*. They prevent injury and discomfort from weld splatter and enable you to pick up the work while it is still hot from welding or cutting. Proper long-sleeved welding gloves are ideal for the job although I must confess I don't like them, preferring ordinary work gloves which are thinner and permit greater sensitivity.

Wear strong clothing such as denim, and your sleeves buttoned up even when the weather is hot. Weld splatter burns on the arms can sometimes be nasty, and I have had quite serious burning from the ultra violet light of the arc (just like sun-burn but it can be a lot worse). Trousers should come down over stout boots and preferably be tied at the ankle. Make sure molten metal can't get in your boots—if it does, it is impossible to remove it quickly enough to avoid painful burns. Leather spats over your boots can solve the problem.

Tools

A *chipping hammer* is the first essential. These come in two sorts so be sure to buy the welder's version, the difference being in the pick which enables the welder to get right into slag traps. An ordinary chipping hammer would also be useful if any rusty metal has to be chipped back to good metal. The chipping hammer should be kept blunt as cuts in the good metal will lead to early corrosion and can seriously diminish the life of the plate.

A *wire brush* will be necessary for cleaning slag out of seams that are being welded. A *cold chisel* may prove useful and a *file* is often handy for finally smoothing off corners after they have been ground. A retractable *metal tape* will be necessary for measuring plate, and an *engineer's rule* will also be useful for transferring angles and transferring measurements from one side of a plate to the other. A *set square* will be worth having and plenty of *french chalk* should be available for marking out the plates.

A good selection of *G-clamps* will complete the tool-bag. The jaws don't need to be very wide, but the deeper they are the better. Special welding 'Mole' clamps are available and these will prove most useful. Clamps can be very easily made by welding ¾ in. square bar into a U and then welding a nut on one end. A bolt with a small bar welded on the top provides the clamping action when screwed through the nut.

12   A home-made G-clamp.

Gas Cutting Gear

I am deliberately ignoring gas welding gear as I do not consider that it has much place in boat construction, the plates being generally too thick. Gas cutting gear, on the other hand, if not essential, is extremely useful on any major project. It comes in two types—oxygen and acetylene or oxygen and propane. Both are equally suited to our purpose, but only oxy-acetylene can be used for welding, as the flame produced by oxy-propane is not sufficiently intense. Propane gas is cheaper than acetylene and the deposit required on the cylinder (all cylinders are hired from the supplying companies and cannot be bought) is considerably less. It is also more readily obtainable. Accordingly, if you are considering gas cutting gear it may be best to go for oxy-propane.

As well as the cylinders you will require bottle gauges, hoses, a cutting gun and a cylinder key. British Oxygen Ltd are the biggest suppliers of gases in Great Britain and their products are readily obtainable all over the country. They are also able to supply the ancillary equipment that may be required. Gauges, hoses and gun are often additionally obtainable through specialist magazines or the Exchange & Mart in Britain at a considerable saving on the leading brands. These should be satisfactory providing they comply with the appropriate safety standards in force. However, you should be careful when buying second-hand equipment unless you can obtain expert advice as to its condition.

The gauge set for each bottle normally consists of two dials and a regulating device. (See photo 13, depicting me with a British Oxygen 'Portapak'.) One will indicate the pressure at which the set is regulated and the other will indicate the contents of the bottle. *An acetylene gauge should not be used on a propane bottle, or vice versa*, as the gauge would be damaged and it could be dangerous. It is essential, therefore, to make sure the gauges are appropriate before you buy. The cutting gun itself also has regulator knobs but these should only be used

13 Mike Pratt with a British Oxygen 'Portapak'.

for fine tuning, the proper pressure being set up on the gauge. Guns come in different sizes and the appropriate one will be determined by the thickness of plate to be cut. Even the smallest gun can be made to cut quite thick plate, it just takes a lot longer. If cutting 4 mm. to 6 mm. is what is normally contemplated, a comparatively light-weight gun would be best as this will be less tiring to use, will economize considerably on gas, and its smaller nozzle will produce a finer, more accurate cut. You also need hoses, but do ensure that those you buy are long enough. Bottles are difficult to move unless you buy a trolley to go with them, so the hoses should be long enough to reach all parts of the job with the bottles sited centrally.

British Oxygen Ltd market a small oxy-acetylene kit

known as 'Portapak'. The whole kit can easily be carried to any work site and could be a useful addition to the maintenance kit of a steel work-boat or even a yacht. The kit consists of small bottles (which are technically leased for ten years), hoses, gauges, and a small gun with a selection of nozzles for both welding and cutting. The gun will cut quite thick plate but the bottles last only a very short time. When cutting, oxygen is used at more than twice the rate of acetylene and the small oxygen bottle will last for only about half an hour's continuous use. The gas comes at a standard price for large or small bottles, as it is the filling of them that costs the money, not the gas itself. Furthermore, British Oxygen puts a standard service charge on every invoice for gas regardless of how many bottles are filled. All this means that buying gas in small quantities is extremely expensive, and cutting done in this way may cost more than if cutting discs are used on the angle-grinder. The ancillary equipment in the kit can, however, be used with large bottles, so if you are undertaking a major project followed by the need for gas for small maintenance jobs, then it may be worth considering. The small bottles cannot be hired independently of the kit. The kit will cost only slightly less than equipment plus the deposit on large bottles, but a small monthly rental is additionally charged on large bottles. The rental is not charged on the small ones.

All gas under pressure can be extremely dangerous, be it in large or small bottles. I have known oxygen bottles take off like a rocket when the cylinder fails, and go soaring way up into the air. Acetylene bottles can explode like a bomb if mistreated or if defective. It is for this reason that the cylinders cannot be bought. They need regular testing, so the suppliers must maintain them under their control in order to see that this is carried out. Propane tends to be less potentially lethal than acetylene but even so its danger should not be under-estimated.

The manufacturers will supply basic safety instructions on request but the following few notes may be useful:

1 Perhaps the biggest danger is a flashback from the gun to the bottles. To prevent this, flame traps should be included somewhere in the line.

2 The acetylene bottle should not be used on its side. Bottles should always be used upright. Dissolved acetylene liquid could run into the valve if the bottle is on its side, and this could be very dangerous.

3 Lash the bottles securely upright when in use. Falling bottles are not only dangerous to people who get in the way, but may cause an explosion.

4 The acetylene bottle should not be allowed to become hot as this may well lead to an explosion. If a bottle does show signs of heating up, work should be immediately stopped, the area cleared, and appropriate authorities called.

5 Don't dust down clothing with compressed oxygen. Oxygen trapped in clothing could be ignited by a spark and cause nasty burning.

6 Always light the gun (acetylene or propane first) with the nozzle pointing away from yourself and other people. Fuel turned accidentally high can shoot a considerable distance with consequent danger to anyone in the way.

7 Guard the hoses against chafe. Leaking fuel may ignite.

8 Turn the cylinders off firmly when work is finished, as leaking gas is not only wasteful, but may cause an explosion. It is a bad habit to switch the gas off just on the regulator, or worse still only at the gun: damage may occur at either or both, especially in transit, and gas will then be allowed to escape. If gas still leaks when the cylinder tap is turned fully home the cylinder should be returned to the supplier for exchange. Do not attempt to

57

force the tap as it could shear off and this will be a potential hazard.

9 It is worth repeating that goggles must always be worn. The bright cutting flame will damage eyes in a very short time and there is also the risk of damage by metal splatter.

If these few basic principles are observed, gas cutting can be comparatively simple and safe. A few hours' practice on scrap plate should allow even the complete beginner to achieve a reasonable degree of competence. The equipment retailer may well be able to arrange for a demonstration, but a brief guide is given here. The pressure gauges should first be set at the level appropriate to the metal thickness and nozzle size. These figures will be given by the equipment manufacturers who often supply them on a card for easy reference. The fuel (acetylene or propane) should then be turned on at the gun and ignited. A reddish yellow smoky flame will result, but it will turn blue as the oxygen is turned on. The flame should be adjusted so that the oxygen and acetylene balance is correct. This is achieved when the

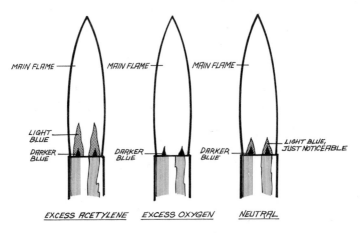

Fig 1 Oxy-acetylene flame adjustment.

lighter blue cones in the flame are adjusted very slightly longer than the darker blue cones (Fig. 1). This is achieved by progressively increasing the oxygen supply. The gun is now ready to cut. The principle is to heat the metal with the flame and then oxidize the hot metal away with a stream of oxygen which is emitted from a hole in the centre of the nozzle by the application of a lever on the gun. Once oxidation has commenced, the work can proceed rapidly as while metal is being oxidized the metal just next to it is in the process of being heated. You may find it helpful to use the gun at a slight angle as in Fig. 2.

DIRECTION OF TRAVEL

Fig 2 Gas cutting.

Practice will improve neatness and increase speed, but cutting is essentially far easier than welding.

The 'Nibbler'

For the amateur I believe that the 'Nibbler' is a much better bet than gas for cutting plate. A sort of electric tin opener, it cuts plate up to $\frac{1}{4}$ in. thick very rapidly without distortion. It is extremely accurate and leaves clean edges ready for welding. (A good one to buy is the Duplux N24 obtainable from J & C (Tools & Accessories) Ltd; at around £250, the machine is not cheap, but there shouldn't be much loss if it is sold at the end of the project.) In any event the investment is only a little greater than that necessary for gas cutting gear with all its inherent distortion problems, and this will not now be required. One 'Nibbler' blade should be sufficient to

14. A 'Nibbler' steel-plate cutter.

cut out a 40-footer and its replacement cost of about £50 will not be far removed from the cost of the equivalent amount of gas.

Cutting discs in the grinder are probably marginally more expensive than either gas or the 'Nibbler'. Even in large quantities it's difficult to get a 9 in. disc for much less than £1.50. As 600 to 800 feet of cutting could be required in a 40-footer, and one disc won't cut much more than 12 feet of $\frac{3}{16}$ in. steel, the total cost would definitely be more than £50. However, the grinder is a necessary piece of equipment anyway, so it doesn't involve additional expense. But it can't be used for cutting out apertures such as portholes and this can be a definite disadvantage.

Mechanical *plate shears* are another alternative and can usually be bought second-hand fairly cheaply. However, in order to move the shears along, the scrap has to be bent. If it is too wide it is difficult to bend and at the same time it is a waste of metal. If you have used tin snips you will know the problem.

Maintenance

The arc-welder and the angle-grinder are extremely robust tools, their only real enemy being water and damp. Provided these are guarded against, no problems should arise. The only regular maintenance normally necessary with the welder will be in connection with the earth and electrode leads, which are prone to fray at the terminals after constant use. Check them often, as slowly diminishing performance caused by poor contacts may otherwise go unnoticed. With gas cutting gear, the gauges are highly susceptible to damage, and should be removed when not in use. They should be stored in protective boxes and their connecting threads must be kept scrupulously clean.

Conclusion

All the tools that have been mentioned should last a very long time, and will be useful for maintenance and fabrication work once the main building or conversion job is finished. Virtually all the gear, with the possible exception of the gas bottles, can be carried aboard the bigger cruising boat, making her largely independent for her repairs. *Abraxis* has a 240/110 volt, 3·0 k.V.A. diesel generator installed for running power tools, making her almost a mobile workshop. The generator has sufficient power to give the welder 100 amperage output, enough to run 14-gauge rods easily and 12's at a push. Most repair jobs can be done with these and patience. *Abraxis*'s generator, made by Allam Generators, Southend, is incidentally extremely compact, and I would thoroughly recommend it to anyone thinking of installing one, especially if space is limited. The Lister predecessor, while a fine machine, was very large and very noisy for its output.

4

Welding is no problem

I read several books on the subject of welding when I first
became involved with steel boats. While they were all very
lucid on the theory of what was supposed to happen, I could
find very little succinct information on the techniques
involved. Consequently my welding remained poor until
Brian Boorman, a qualified welder friend, pointed out a few
simple things I was doing wrong. Since then my welding has
improved in leaps and bounds and practice has led to con-
tinued improvement. I do not advocate an in-depth theoretical study of welding for the would-be steel boat-builder.
Much better to work on as many types of job as possible. It
quickly becomes easy to tell while you are welding whether or
not the resulting join will be satisfactory. In this chapter I
shall simply pass on the tips that Brian showed to me, and I
believe that with plenty of practice you will quickly discover
that welding is no problem.

The first essential is to select a suitable brand of rod. I
experimented with many and eventually settled on Oerlikon
yellow tip, an all-positional rod with which it is very easy to
strike and maintain an arc. Rods come in different sizes and
lengths according to the type of job for which they are
required. Size is measured in s.w.g. or millimetres. The
smaller the s.w.g. figure the larger the rod. For our purposes
16 s.w.g. to 8 s.w.g. will be useful, 16 being the smallest size
that is made. The following table gives an approximate
indication of rod usage in relation to plate thickness, together
with a note as to the amperage at which the welder should
be set.

Plate thickness inches	Rod	Amperage	Runs
$\frac{1}{8}$	12	100	1
	14	60	1—possibly more
$\frac{3}{16}$	12	100	1
	14	60	Several
$\frac{1}{4}$	10	130	1—if you are lucky
	12	100	Several
$\frac{3}{8}$	8	180	Not really suitable for small machines
	10	130	1—probably more
	12	100	Several

NOTE: Amperages are approximate depending on conditions and types of rod. These amperages are slightly high by manufacturer's recommended standards, but I have found that most professional welders have the power turned well up. Whilst I am far from being a professional I have found through experience that this is advantageous.

For special applications I find SAF or Philips rods to be extremely good. The following table indicates types of rod suitable for different applications:

Application	Type of Rod	
	SAF	PHILIPS
Mild Steel		
All positions and vertical going down	G48N	42
All positions	G47	53
Vertical going down	L51	37 or 39

Application	Type of Rod	
	SAF	PHILIPS
Stainless Steel		
Stainless steel + stainless steel ⎱	Safinox 18–8	Inox IR
Stainless steel + mild steel ⎰	RCN 29–10	80
Stainless steel + special steel ⎱	RCN 29–10	80
Stainless steel + unknown steel ⎰		

Any of the stainless rods would be all right for welding special steels such as Cor-Ten, with the Philips 80 being especially good, but expensive. Oerlikon also make electrodes for special applications.

The length of rod will be determined by the lengths of run to be completed and by the experience of the welder. It is easier to control a shorter rod, so the beginner should use 12 in. rods until his skill increases. Indeed, longer rods are seldom necessary as even on plating jobs long runs should be avoided because of the danger of distortion.

Before you start to weld, ensure that the negative lead from the welder has a good earth on to the work. Poor earth contact is the most frequent cause of difficulty in striking an arc. It is also worth repeating here that protective clothing must be worn including gloves, boots, and tough shirts (buttoned down to the gloves) and jeans. Remember to protect your eyes by using a helmet or shield.

The basic theory of 'stick' welding is not difficult. The arc from the electrode (positive lead from the welder) is used to melt the two pieces of metal to be joined (metal being connected to the negative lead from the welder), and the gap is filled by molten metal from the electrode itself. The electrode is covered in flux which, amongst other things, excludes oxygen from the weld which would otherwise diminish the strength.

In order to obtain a satisfactory result it is essential to concentrate on the weld totally. A fraction of a second's

64

inattention can lead to the electrode tip wandering, thus allowing the weld to cool and a flaw to result. Concentrating on the arc can be very tiring and I have often ended up with a headache after a long day's welding, especially when I was beginning.

To practice, obtain some 12 s.w.g. electrodes (which are a useful size for many jobs) together with some scrap pieces of ⅛ in. plate. Set the latter up in a vice and thoroughly clean the edges to be welded. Then, after ensuring that no-one else is looking in the direction of the arc, first try to put a run of weld down the plate. The position of the rod in the holder is important and should be at an angle to the work as in Fig. 3.

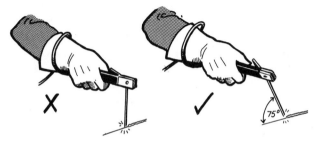

Fig 3 Welding: positioning of rod in holder.

If the rod is held vertically to the work, the slag (flux and impurities) is prevented from bubbling away behind the weld as it progresses and there is a risk of slag being trapped in the weld thereby producing a fault. It is also important not to grip the electrode holder too tightly as this will cause tenseness which makes it very difficult to control the tip of the rod adequately.

There is a temptation to try and strike the arc poking at the plate with a stabbing motion. This should be avoided as it often results in the flux coating being damaged, which makes it very difficult to weld until the rod has been burnt down to good flux. Instead you should stroke the plate at right angles to the direction of the joint. This should result in an immediate arc, and if not, it probably means that either the earth or welder connections are loose or the rod is imperfect. Rods suffer heavily if exposed to damp conditions and are often difficult to light and to use if this has happened. A solution is to warm the rods in an oven, but this can result in the coating becoming brittle. Sometimes a used rod will have slag solidified on its end, especially if it has become excessively hot in use. Here is one instance when it will have to be stabbed at the plate in order to get a good contact. However, this should be done away from the work, and the job recommenced when contact has been achieved.

When working along a joint it is necessary to weave the rod to ensure a strong weld. The pattern should be kept as regular as possible for a neat job, and it is important not to go back over the track. For example, you should avoid going round in circles, as in Fig. 4, as this goes over the top of the slag, thereby locking imperfections (slag and blow holes) in the weld. But the pattern marked with a tick is by no means the only acceptable version.

Fig 4 Welding patterns.

One of the greatest problems the beginner finds is that of maintaining the rod at the right distance from the work. Too far away will result in a splatter-type surface weld and the risk of losing the arc, whereas too near causes the arc to dig into the plate (undercutting) and consequently an uneven weld. If the arc is lost, it is essential to stop and chip and brush the weld, as the slag will have been given a chance to solidify. Starting up again immediately will result in slag being locked in. The correct distance from the plate will depend on a number of factors such as plate thickness and type of rod and it is normally necessary to experiment before starting the job proper. One quarter inch or so will normally be too far and the result will be metal deposited on the surface with no real penetration. One eighth inch or less should ensure adequate penetration and consequently a much stronger job. The following weld profiles illustrate these principles:

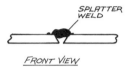

FRONT VIEW

Fig 5 Inadequate weld penetration. CAUSE: Amperage too low or rod held too far away.

15 Faulty weld profile. FAULT: Dips in the welded joint below the level of the plate. CAUSE: Amperage too high or rod held too near.

FRONT VIEW

Fig 6 Sound weld, has penetrated through to underside of plate and at the top blends into the plate without undercutting.

The beginner often finds that it is all too easy to burn holes in the plate that is being welded. Filling holes can be a tedious business so all precautions should be taken to avoid them. They normally result from inattention and concentrating the arc for too long in one spot, or possibly having the welder set at too high an amperage. If a hole does occur, the procedure is to try and deposit metal around the edge without applying too much heat which would make the problem worse. The amperage should be turned down to reduce the heat and the impact of the arc. It will be necessary to stop frequently in order to allow the area to cool, and each time the weld will need to be chipped and brushed.

Downhand or horizontal welding is the easiest of all positions but this is seldom found in on-site boat construction. Most welds will be at some angle, and while a slight slope will not complicate the job significantly, vertical welding does cause problems for the novice. It is possible to work either upwards or downwards, but the former is normally easier. When going up, the slag is carried away from the weld by gravity, unfortunately there is also a tendency for the deposited metal to behave in the same way. This results in beads hanging down which look unsightly and can lead to imperfections. The beads can be ground away and a second run put over the joint although this is time-consuming. The only answer here is practice, and in time you will discover the knack of going sufficiently fast to prevent the metal from beading, but not so fast that imperfections result. Working downwards can be useful especially on thin plate or in confined conditions. Here you have to increase the rate of

68

working, so as to keep ahead of the slag flowing down on top of the weld, and the faster speed could result in poor penetration. To counteract this tendency it will be necessary to increase the amperage by around 20 per cent. This method does not deposit much metal, but a reasonable fast weld can be achieved.

Overhead welding is only a little more difficult than downhand once the awkward stance has been mastered. Indeed it is the awkward welding pose that causes problems here and not technical difficulty. The slag is carried away from the weld by gravity and the real task is to stand in such a position as to avoid being splashed by molten metal. Amperage will be slightly higher than for downhand welding and the rod may be held almost at a right angle to the work (unlike downhand where we saw that a 75 degree angle was necessary).

I mentioned at the beginning of this chapter that it would soon become easy to tell whether a weld is satisfactory or not. This is done by watching how the molten metal cools. A bright fiery red, sometimes with sparks in it, indicates a flaw in the weld whereas a deeper duller red indicates a satisfactory job. The fault will take longer to cool off than the sound weld so a point that remains bright red after the rest has cooled will need thorough chipping to remove the slag. The cooling process takes only a few seconds but the faults are readily identified with a little experience. And as experience grows, the number of faults should decrease, but when they do occur all slag must be removed before the area is rewelded. Chipping will normally do it, but it may be necessary to use a pick to clean up the flaw. In certain circumstances flaws can be eradicated by increasing the amperage and welding over the top. The greater heat can cause the slag to rise to the top but there is a risk of trapping slag in the weld so I would not advocate this method for any joints that must be perfectly watertight.

A basic knowledge of butt and angled joints should be sufficient for most small-boat construction. With any joint the preparation of the plate edge is critical, and the angle-grinder should be used on flame-cut plate to fair off the edge. When butt joints are being welded the grinder should be used to V off the edges as in Fig. 7. This is best done for all plate even down to as thin as 3 mm.

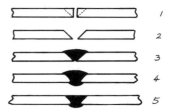

Fig 7 Edge preparation.

As in the diagrams, a gap should be left between the plates to allow proper penetration and help prevent the possibility of buckling. One run should be sufficient on 4 mm. plate, but a second run on the reverse side is preferable to ensure perfect penetration and complete watertightness (step 4). It is then possible to grind off the surface weld to make a smooth surface (step 5).

The standard of the overall finish will be governed by your success in preventing buckling of the plates. Buckling is caused by excessive localized heat distorting the plate. A useful technique to help prevent this is as follows:

1 Tack the plates together at about 50 cm. intervals.
2 Tack angle bar across the join as in Fig. 8.

Fig 8 Preventing distortion at the join.

Flat bar can be used for this purpose provided it has a perfectly straight edge, but angle is stronger. The angle bar should be tacked on one side only as it is then easy to break off on completion of welding by knocking against the tacks.

3 Welding straight along the join will increase the risk of distortion, so the technique of back-step welding should be used as in Fig. 9.

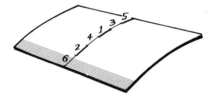

Fig 9 Back-step welding.

The length of each step will vary according to conditions, particularly the thickness of the plate. On 4 mm. plate 18 cm. would be reasonable. It is best practice to work from the centre of the plate outwards.

With thick plate one run may be insufficient even if it is chamfered and large rods are being used. The rod/amperage table on page 63 gives an indication of runs necessary, but this will vary with conditions. Plate of 12mm. is likely to be the thickest in common use and here it may be necessary to build up the weld as in Fig. 10, using three runs:

Fig 10 Fillet-weld using three runs.

Alternatively one run may be put in the bottom of the V and a broad run then put over the top, as in Fig. 11:

Fig 11 Fillet-weld using two runs.

Joints where the plates are set at an angle to each other are more difficult to achieve, as the action of welding tends to draw the two pieces away from their required relationship. Normally the thinner or less well-secured plate will be drawn in the direction of the other.

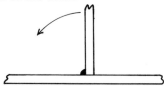

Welding along one side of this angle joint will tend to pull the vertical plate in the direction of the arrow.

Fig 12 Weld distortion.

To prevent this distortion it is necessary to tack on either side of the joint ensuring that as little heat as possible is applied. When the tacking is complete the joint should be welded in a sequence similar to that in Fig. 13:

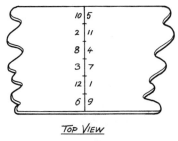

Fig 13 Welding sequence.

If the vertical plate is sizeable and no framing is involved it may be necessary to triangulate the joint by tacking angle bar to both plates as in Fig. 14, the tacking to be on one side only so as to facilitate breaking when the welding is complete.

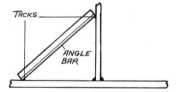

Fig 14 Triangulating a joint before welding.

There is always a danger of undercutting when welding angled joints and all precautions should be taken against this as it can seriously weaken the job.

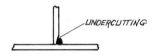

Fig 15 Undercutting.

Careful attention to the amperage (which may be slightly lower than normal) and concentration on the arc should avoid the problem.

One run a side may be insufficient on plate thicker than 5mm. In this case the procedure is similar to that with butt joints with multiple runs as in Fig. 16:

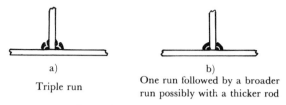

a)

Triple run

b)

One run followed by a broader run possibly with a thicker rod

Fig 16 Right-angle joints.

Avoid overwelding as this will create a stress point which could lead to an ultimate fracture.

73

Summary

The techniques described in this chapter will be sufficient to make a good strong job of the types of joint likely to be encountered in small-boat construction work. For those who like practical instruction, night-school welding classes are available in many cities and several big companies have a welding school.

In conclusion, however, I re-emphasize that practice is the key to success.

5

Steel Construction Systems

There are probably as many different systems for putting a
steel boat together as there are builders, but it is possible to
identify five basic structures:

> Single chine
> Multi-chine
> Rounded chine
> Strip chine
> Round bilge

These five possibilities can be extended by the fact that with
any type of chine-building there is a choice between *framed*
and *monocoque* construction, thereby increasing the number of
permutations to nine. With each one of these permutations
there are several different possible sequences of building. I'm
going to have a look at the relative merits of each type of
structure, to compare framed with frameless construction,
and then assess the best building sequence for the first-time
amateur.

Single Chine

Single chine has the merit of being a very simple form of
construction, permitting the use of mostly flat plates. This
method was used for the building of both *Steelaway* and *Avalon*
(photos 5 and 7) and can provide a boat with entirely satisfactory sailing qualities. It is, however, imperative that the
design takes account of the water flow around the hull, and is
not simply produced on the basis of building convenience.
The chines must be set in the true lines of the water flow so as
to minimize the resistance that turbulence at the chines may

16 From the META shipyard. 'Embrun', a single-chine version of
Joshua, designed for amateur construction.

create, the turbulence being produced where the flow crosses
the chine at an angle. Unfortunately, the water-flow pattern
will tend to change at various angles of heel, so that the boat
will only tend to sail at its best at one specific angle. Sail
trimming can accordingly become that much more critical
with a chine boat, be it single- or multi-chine.

If single chine is to be used, then I believe that a fine entry
is essential to prevent the boat slamming in a seaway. A
broad entry with chines such as in photo 17 will probably
cause an uncomfortable motion through slamming, and
make the boat slow as she will have to push a wall of water
along in front.

Only tank testing will really reveal whether a design has
actually got the chines in the right place, and this process is,
of course, expensive and, therefore, comparatively rare. One
design that we discovered on a recent trip to Holland had
received this treatment and the results were impressive. The
designer, Kees Koopman, and the builders, Scheepswerf De
Rietpol, Spaarndam, had put considerable effort into creat-

17 A broad entry with chines is unsatisfactory.

ing a 32ft. or 38ft. multi-chine bilge-keeler that would really
sail. The expense of tank testing was high so they are under-
standably reluctant to release the plans, but they do produce
the hull and decks at a competitive price and both are very
roomy boats finished to a high standard.

Many British chine steel designs have evolved from
plywood originals, the only attempt at design testing being
empirically, at the expense of the poor owner after he has
completed his boat and found that it doesn't sail. Some
designers are worse than others in this respect, but it may be
useful to chat to an existing owner before committing oneself
to a set of plans.

Multi-Chine

The term *Multi-chine* refers to the situation where two or more
chines are introduced in the design, the chines adding considerably to the boat's strength. To the extent that this
produces more angles, improperly designed multi-chiners
may actually create more resistance than their single-chine
counterparts. This should not normally be so, however, in

77

18 Robert Tucker's pretty multi-chine 'Turanna'. The chine plates fair in so as to be scarcely noticeable above the waterline.

that the multi-chine will enable the use of less acute angles and correspondingly there will be less likelihood of turbulence. The multi-chines must still follow the water-flow lines and the angle of sailing will still be critical, as an increase in angle of heel may well produce an increase in resistance totally disproportionate to the greater wetted surface.

The multi-chine boat does have other advantages over the single-chine version beside the less acute chine angles and consequent probable reduction in turbulence. The increased number of chines will help to produce a more curvaceous and perhaps, therefore, more attractive hull. Additionally, it will be possible to create a deeper-bodied vessel, thereby giving greater headroom the lack of which can be a problem in smaller chined craft.

Rounded Chine
Turbulence at the chines can be reduced by using a technique which we can conveniently call *Rounded-chine*. That is, instead of having a hard knuckle where the plates join, a 'soft chine' is created by one of a number of means. The simplest way is to use either round bar or tube of fairly large diameter welded into the chine, as in Fig. 17:

78

Fig 17 Tubular chine bar.

Round bar is to be preferred, as it can be ground down if necessary and is not subject to rusting from the inside as is the case with tube. In either case there is considerable advantage over the hard chine in reduced turbulence, increased strength, and the fact that rounded corners hold their paint better than sharp corners. The problems are the extra time involved in welding, and the increased weight. The latter will not usually be significant, but the former may be unless the boat is being amateur-built with no strict timetable.

A more sophisticated rounded chine can be obtained by using flat plates but leaving a gap at the chines. This gap can then be filled by narrow plates which will have to be specially rolled. This type of construction could be attractive to the amateur builder, as the comparatively small task of rolling could be contracted out quite cheaply. Quite a curvaceous hull can be achieved in this way, although normally a fairly slack bilge will result. See photos 19 and 20 overleaf. The bilge and topside plates have very slight curve in them, but this can be put in manually. The chine plate will need to be rolled but the garboard plate could simply meet the keel at an angle as indicated. It is not worth leaving a gap at this point to be filled by rolled plate. If this angle joint doesn't appeal, it may be better to fill in the angle with thin plate which will not be structural. Alternatively, the angle could be faired in with mesh and ferro-cement used to produce a smooth curve, as in

79

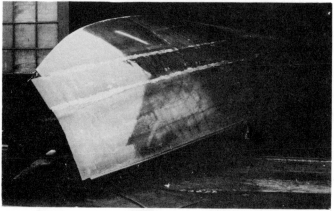

19 and 20 A rounded chine using flat plates but leaving
a gap at the chines.

Fig. 18. If plate is used, a hollow section will be produced in
which rust could form. To prevent this, the section could be
drilled then filled with oil, pitch or expanded foam.

The only problem with this method of rounded-chine con-

Fig 18 Mesh and
cement for fairing in.

struction is that it is difficult to produce a deep-displacement
boat with firm sections. Either fairly flat bilge plates and
consequent relatively shallow draft or slack sections must be
accepted. I don't like slack sections from an aesthetic point of
view but, worse, they can make the boat very tender. Shallow
draft, though, can be a positive advantage if there is sufficient
beam to give initial stability. Headroom, however, is always
a problem in smaller boats built like this, but no more so than
with chined versions. A lot of tophamper may have to be
introduced to gain sufficient headroom but this need not be
obtrusive if the design is appropriate. A useful technique is to
have the boat flush-decked with some tumblehome to take off
the boxy appearance. If the top line of plates is painted a
contrasting colour the result can be most attractive. *Avalon*, a
Dutch professionally built centre-boarder, and *Steelaway*, an
amateur built conventional keel boat (photos 7 and 5) are
both built with this system. *Avalon* has an attractive pro-
nounced sheer accentuated by a contrasting paint-scheme
that makes what could have been a boxy boat into something
most attractive. *Steelaway* has less sheer but more tumblehome, a fraction too much of the latter according to the
owner, but again, the combination is an appealing one. The
result in both boats is a very roomy interior with ample
headroom despite shallow draft.

Strip Chine
The Strip-chine method has many advantages from the

81

amateur builder's point of view. In this approach the topside and bottom plates of the hull are joined by a strip of constant width which is usually of slightly thicker steel than the rest of the hull. In this way the benefits of multi-chine are gained without the complexity of cutting out chine plates which taper towards the ends. Cutting can be minimized by obtaining plate of the appropriate width (usually between six inches and one foot) in long lengths so that the entire chine plate can be fitted at one go. If plate can't be bought in long enough lengths, then the shorter strips should be welded up on the bench before plating begins.

The chine plate is normally the first to go up, and as such provides an excellent fair line against which to butt the rest of the plating. As an additional bonus, if the thicker plate is used (say $\frac{1}{4}$ in.), the need for chine stringers may be obviated, thus saving considerable welding time. Since the chine strips should run easily, they will give a good indication of whether any of the frames are out of true. Frames which are out can then be adjusted before plating proper commences. This type of construction is usually frameless (see p. 83) so that the boat will be built on a jig consisting of mock frames which are subsequently discarded.

Round Bilge

The remaining option is the traditional *Round-bilge* craft such as our own *Abraxis* (see photo 6) or Bernard Moitessier's famous *Joshua*. Such boats can feature firm sections and deep draft with heavily curved plates at the turn of the bilge (see photo 37). These plates will normally require rolling, so that this method of construction is often regarded as beyond the ability of the average amateur builder. This need not necessarily be so, as 4mm. plate can be curved by a variety of means, e.g. using tackles, Acrojacks, hydraulic rams (used for car repairs), heating or power hammering (more about all this later). Nowadays 4mm. is considered entirely satisfactory for boats up to 50 feet. The Hiscocks' *Wanderer IV* is made from this thickness, and Dr. David Lewis's famous *Ice Bird* was made from even thinner—3mm. Personally, I prefer a bit more margin for error and like to see bilge plating of 6mm., but I am old-fashioned in this respect. As far as strength is concerned, the thinner plate is undoubtedly more than sufficient, but corrosion can quickly condemn it. And thicker plating below the waterline contributes towards ballast and stability anyway.

In any event the round-bilge method is undoubtedly far more time-consuming and my feeling is that it is dated as far as steel construction is concerned. It has persisted with steel because few designs have been created with an eye to the material's own special construction advantages and needs. But this is all changing, and it would be a properly designed chine boat that I would go for now.

Framed and Frameless Construction

If a chine boat has been decided upon, a further choice has to be made between framed or frameless construction. Entirely satisfactory frameless craft are commonly built in Holland in sizes up to 40 feet, and the method has much to commend it. Weight-saving is an obvious plus, but time may be saved as well, if an appropriate building sequence is chosen (see p. 86). Additionally, internal maintenance of the hull can be considerably simplified if frames are done away with. Preparation can be done using power tools over uninterrupted smooth surfaces, and the risk of missing nooks and crannies, either with preparation or painting, is minimized. A marginal advantage is the internal space saving that the lack of frames gives, but against this, I would prefer to tack angle to the frame rather than directly to plate during the course of furniture construction. Finally, the biggest plus of all, frames are a real rust trap—water trapped by a frame in *Abraxis* caused a plate to be eaten away from the inside and its

21 Frameless construction in a Robert Tucker 38-footer.

complete replacement was necessary. It is a well-known fact that steel boats often rust away from the inside and not from the outside. With frameless boats denting can be a problem if too thin plate is used, so it is common practice to use comparatively thick steel at least for the bilge plating. I would view 6mm. as being a minimum, and much thicker could be used and regarded as part of the ballast. Alternatively concrete can be poured into the bottom of the boat as ballast and to prevent denting. I believe that it is inadvisable to go below 4mm. for topside plating, again for fear of denting, but many smaller boats are built in Holland out of less and without frames. Such boats are common in hire fleets there, as they are cheap to buy and maintain. And in common with all the boats in Holland's crowded waterways, they have to face frequent bumping in the locks and from the many laden barges. Often in the hands of unskilled charterers, these little craft take quite heavy punishment in their stride, which says much for this method of construction.

With traditional framed construction the sequence of building would be much the same whether the boat is to be round-bilge or chined. With chine, however, the frame fabrication is very much easier as less bending will be necessary. The boat may be built upside down (photo 22) or the right way up; or in a sophisticated yard, the hull may be built inside a rotating hoop arrangement which enables the job to be turned to the most convenient point of access (see photo 37), thereby facilitating mostly downhand welding. Without heavy lifting gear the amateur will have to build right side up, but this should be no real disadvantage. First the keel will be built, normally from heavy plate built up into a box section. To this will be added a strongback to form the basis of framing. Next the stem and transom framework will be added and bulkheads installed. The framework could next be welded up and the deckbeams installed to give the whole structure rigidity. Plating up is by no means a gentle business

22 Building upside down to a John Teale design.

so the framework has to be very solid before this stage commences. One way to achieve greater rigidity in the structure is to weld on the decks before starting to plate. This idea has a lot to commend it as the plates will lie naturally to the camber on the decks and any curve required will be in one plane only. Consequently plating up the deck will be a speedy process and will add considerably to the framework strength. Even if the boat is not to be flush-decked (I think she should be, as construction is considerably simplified and in my view the result is stronger and more seamanlike), it may pay to plate right across and then cut out plate as necessary for any coachroofs or hatches. The deckplating will give an edge against which to butt up the plates, the fitting of which should now be a relatively routine matter.

With frameless construction, the traditional way to build is by first constructing a set of moulds upon which the hull is then built upside down. The mould construction will take some time, and unless a series of boats is to be built to the same design there is little advantage in this method. A number of building sequences are possible without moulds, but the one that appealed to me most from those we saw on our trip to Holland in the summer of 1977 was that shown to us by the Scheepswerf De Rietpol. Starting with the bilge plating, they first weld in the floors then turn the plates upside down so that the outside seams may be welded downhand. The bilge keels are then welded on prior to turning the embryo hull back the right way up. This done, the stem and bulkheads are welded in together with the transom and then the decks are fitted. The plate shapes are taken from the lofting floor and welded up to the decks and down to the bilge plating. The multi-chine method gives the plating rigidity while building is under way. The whole process is very rapid and enables the yard to produce a 38ft. hull comparatively cheaply, especially when the high labour costs in Holland are taken into account. A 38ft. round-bilge steel hull for sale at

De Rietpol at the same time as the bilge-keeler of the same length cost precisely twice as much, even though she was of much narrower beam and much smaller inside. This aptly illustrates the vastly increased time that is necessary for the construction of round-bilge boats, and this for a yard well versed in their production.

Frameless chine boats can be produced very rapidly by amateurs as well. The 32ft. *Steelaway* was built by ex-owner Tony Porter and a professional steelworker in the rapid time of six weeks.

One problem of building in steel is that of finding appropriate designs. The design often dictates the method of construction. Unless you have a long time to spend building, I would choose a design that is based on the use of chines.

6

Selecting Steel Plans

'There would be a lot more steel boats built by amateurs if more designers had worked with the material earlier,' says Bruce Roberts in his helpful introductory booklet for amateur builders called *Build for Less*. I agree with him. There has been a dearth of good designs drawn specifically for steel construction, and steel designs aimed at the amateur have been virtually unobtainable until comparatively recently. Even now there are only a few designers who have had real experience with the material. This is all changing, though, and we are now seeing a revolution in amateur building comparable to the plywood revolution of the early sixties. Bruce Roberts International have stopped selling ferro plans and concentrate on steel, plywood and GRP. Robert Tucker told me recently that over two-thirds of their work for some time now has been in steel. In Holland, of course, they can't understand why it has taken us so long to see the light.

In the booklet mentioned above, Bruce Roberts says, 'I am now a little bigoted on the subject and believe that steel has great merit as far as the amateur is concerned.' Robert Tucker, likewise, is very enthusiastic about the material, and said to me that he regards ferro-cement with 'a great deal of circumspection'. As he says, when they are good, ferro boats are very, very good, but the quality control necessary is such that when they are bad they are disastrous.

But perhaps I am preaching to the converted. It's now time to select the plans. I have concentrated this survey on sailboats in the 26ft. to 45ft. range. I believe that beyond 45 feet, although the hull could be produced cheaply enough in steel, the fitting-out costs become just too prohibitive. I don't believe it worth building much below 26 feet as there will be little difference in building time between a 20-footer and a 26-footer, and the cost difference of the material involved is minimal. Nor should the fitting out costs be significantly different.

Hull weight used to be a problem in little boats, but this is no longer a real difficulty as the design can be for frameless construction using the chines for strength and thereby considerably reducing the weight. So tiny steel boats *can* be built if anyone particularly wants to.

In my design selections which follow I deliberately exclude accommodation plans, for reasons I explain on p. 201.

There are probably more boats being built by amateurs to Bruce Roberts designs than to those of any other designer. It's easy to see why. His booklet *Build for Less* features details of all his designs plus advice on material and design selection, all put together in a very readable package. The plan package demonstrates the same professionalism. Plans consist of around 30 sheets of drawings and include full-size patterns of hull frames, stem, etc., and incorporate many drawings of how fittings can be manufactured cheaply. Mr Roberts has aimed fairly and squarely at the amateur market and believes in guiding the amateur builder step by step through each operation. He says 'The builder should be taken from the very first step right through to the launching stage and nothing should be left out; the amateur should not have to make too many decisions for himself. It is in these areas that some of the mistakes are made that cause some boats to turn out less successful than they otherwise might have been if the amateur had a thorough plan which would leave nothing to doubt.' There are many Roberts designs to choose from all based on the multi-chine configuration and they all demonstrate the clean, sleek lines that I find very attractive. The following are my particular favourites:

Fig 19 Roberts 34.　　　　　Fig 20 Roberts Offshore 38b.

Fig 21 Roberts Spray 40.　　　Fig 22 Roberts Mauritius 43.

Roberts 34— LOA 33′6″, Beam 10′3″, Draft 5′6″
Offshore 38B—LOA 38′3″, Beam 11′3″, Draft 5′7″
Spray 40— LOA 40′, Beam 14′4″, Draft 4′2″
Mauritius 43—LOA 43′3″, Beam 13′, Draft 6′

The '38B' is one I would definitely consider if I were to build anew, although I must admit I would be asking Bruce Roberts if there was any way of converting her to schooner rig as I'm not much fond of the ketch. Plans cost (in 1978) from approximately £280 for the 34 to around £360 for the 43.

Robert Tucker has a number of steel designs to choose from, and I have included a selection covering our size range. Mr Tucker's plans are as cheap as any, although paper patterns aren't provided as with Bruce Roberts' package. As Tony Tucker said to me, 'patterns can cause more problems than they solve'. Even if the patterns are reproduced extremely accurately, they can distort very easily with damp and it is very easy to transpose the lines incorrectly. Tables of offsets are by no means as difficult to understand as beginners often believe, and lofting shouldn't be too much of a problem. Nevertheless patterns can do much to cut down time in construction, and provided they are treated with caution and used in conjunction with offset tables, I am in favour of them.

The Tucker family has a wealth of information with regard to building in steel, and they are very prepared to chat and give advice whenever it is needed. If one of their designs should be to your taste, this kind of back-up could prove very useful, especially if you are building for the first time.

Beagle—LOA 28′6″, Beam 11′5″, Draft 3′6″, Sail 397ft.[2]
RW31— LOA 31′4″, Beam 12′4″, Draft 4′, Sail 460ft.[2]
R383— LOA 37′8″, Beam 11′6″, Draft 4′, Sail 640ft.[2]
Vamos—As R383 but Schooner-rigged
Scylla 45—LOA 44′, Beam 12′, Draft 6′, Sail 725ft.[2]
Turanna—LOA 51′4″, Beam 15′6″, Draft 6′5″, Sail 906ft.[2]

Fig 23 Tucker Beagle.   Fig 24 Tucker RW31.

Fig 25 Tucker R383.   Fig 26 Tucker Scylla 45.

Fig 27 Tucker Turanna.

Alan Pape has an extremely attractive traditional design for a cruising ketch, with most of the right ingredients for me—long straight keel, centre cockpit, clipper bow and a very pretty sheer. A shame about the ketch bit . . . She is a big boat at 45 feet overall, with a healthy beam of 12ft. 9in., and a draft of 6ft. 6in., sail area 825ft.^{2}. Construction is a multi-chine, using frames and chine bars.

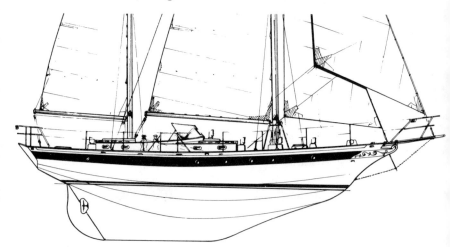

Fig 28 Pape Ketch.

Two Maurice Griffiths designs are available in steel from Bruce Roberts (UK) Ltd. The 37-footer, 'Francis Drake', is a larger version of one of Mr Griffiths' most popular designs, the 'Golden Hind 31'. The 'Francis Drake' hull is double-chined and features a trough keel plus bilge keels. With only 4ft. 3in. draft, the 'Francis Drake' is ideal for gunk-holing around, and if it is anything like its smaller cousin which has at least 25 Atlantic crossings to its credit, it should be well suited to ocean voyaging as well. By modern standards the beam is extremely narrow at 9ft. 7½in. on a waterline of nearly

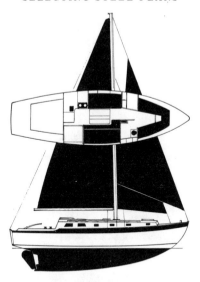

Fig 29 Griffiths Levanter 33.

30 feet, making her a relatively small boat for her size. Maurice Griffiths perhaps realized this and has recently produced a new steel design based on the '37' and called 'Levanter 33'. This 33ft. 6in. overall cutter has a 10ft. 1in. beam which seems a much better beam/length relationship, although by no means extreme. Like the '37', she is shoal draft, at 4 feet, and has the same trough keel plus optional bilge keel, and the accommodation plan is very similar. This is a particular favourite of mine, and one I would strongly recommend. Plans cost (in 1978) about £200.

Peter Ibold's 'Endurance' range is best known built in ferro-cement, but two of the designs, the '35' and the '44', are available for amateur construction in steel. The price of the plans is competitive. Both boats are built on a transversal system with round-bilge sections as opposed to the much easier to construct multi-chine. Endurances have, however,

Fig 30 Ibold Endurance 44.

been built in steel by amateurs although the job is likely to take up to twice as long as for an equivalent multi-chine design. This is evidenced by the fact that at the time of writing, an 'Endurance 44' hull and deck built by Arma Marine of Brightlingsea (who specialize in this design) costs about twice as much as the Bruce Roberts 'Mauritius 43' of comparable size, but built in multi-chine. The 'Endurance 44' is a fine ship though, for those who have the time and skill.

Jean Knocker's *Joshua* is famous for the many incredible voyages made by her owner Bernard Moitessier who commissioned her for world voyaging. *Joshua* is of round-bilge construction and is available from shipyard META to any stage of completion in any of seven different configurations. Many of this design can now be seen around the world used as voyaging homes, but it is an exceptional amateur who could complete the round-bilged, canoe-sterned hull to a satisfactory standard. However, META do provide a very complete service for amateur steel-builders in France, and market two chine designs by modern French designers, specifically aimed at the amateur market. In addition, they provide a complete back-up service including advice on all aspects of construction and corrosion protection. These hulls are very powerful and attractive, and feature the flush deck that I like so much. The 'Embrun' (in French this means 'Spray') is modelled on the lines of *Joshua*, but with simple single-chine construction. A big boat this, with all the desirable features for a cruising home—aft separate sleeping accommodation is included, with a large galley and chart room centrally situated, together with separate living area and plenty of room for stowage.

The slightly smaller 'Defer' is also an attractive proposition, making a great family cruiser or long distance voyager. Her 10ft. 9in. beam on a 29ft. 6in. LOA allows for a roomy interior incorporating walk-in galley and separate sit-down chart table, together with a cosy living area. And the flush deck gives plenty of safe working space.

Vital statistics of the META boats are as follows:

Embrun—LOA 39′8″, Beam 12′, Draft 6′, Sail 700ft.[2]
Defer—LOA 29′6″, Beam 10′9″, Draft 5′2″, Sail 400ft.[2]

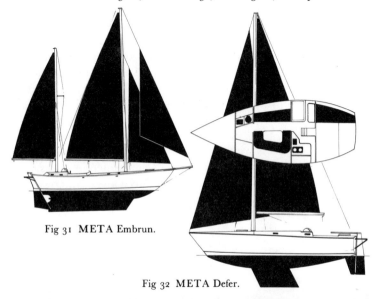

Fig 31 META Embrun.

Fig 32 META Defer.

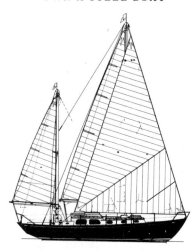

Fig 33 Mason S87.

The Americans have not done very much in steel, but a couple of designs have caught my attention. The Al Mason 'S-87' 41-footer is particularly attractive, but how much is due to the beauty of the design and how much to Mason's incredible draftsmanship I'm not sure. The 'S-87' is certainly a remarkable boat as it features all developed surfaces, which allows for the use of flat plates of steel with no compound curvature while at the same time producing an attractively shaped hull. Despite the after cockpit, Mr Mason has achieved a cabin aft of the main saloon, and without an unsightly dog-house. I am a centre cockpit fan, but for those who like after cockpits the tasteful hull shape and pretty sheer make this powerful cruising yacht an interesting proposition. A 33ft. version is also available without the after cabin.

Jay Benford is well known for his character ferro-cement boats. Unfortunately he hasn't done very much in steel sailboats. However, he has recently produced a very interesting

Fig 34 Benford 40 Brigantine.

40ft. brigantine steel design aimed at the amateur builder. A real character boat this one, and I love the rig, which is just like that of *Abraxis* except we haven't got any yards crossed—yet!

Van de Stadt is probably the best known Dutch designer in England, having designed such famous GRP boats as the 'Westerly' range and the 'Trintellas'. A comprehensive range of multi-chine steel boats is also available, from the 'Zeebonk' at 8·70 metres to the 'Zeelust' at 13·0 metres. The designs are all modern in appearance and mostly feature the fin and skeg configuration. The 'Zeebonk' plans are very cheap, but those of the 'Zeelust' extremely expensive, and in my opinion this latter is not so interesting as many of the 40ft. designs which we have already looked at. The following is a selection covering the range:

Zeebonk—LOA 8·70m, Beam 2·90., Draft 1·50m., Sail 47·3m.[2]

97

Fig 35 Van de Stadt Zeebonk.

Zeehond—LOA 11·00m., Beam 3·54m., Draft 1·90m., Sail 79·5m.[2]

Zeelust—LOA 13·00m., Beam 3·90m., Draft 1·90m., Sail 118·0m.[2]

I have often been asked if there are any round-bilge plans available that are suitable for use by builders with only limited experience in steelwork. There are. The 'Table Bay 39' and the 'Tahitiana' come into this category, and at 39 feet and 32 feet respectively, these two boats are aimed fairly and squarely at the blue-water sailor. Dream ships these, and I would be happy to own either of them.

'Table Bay 39' is based on the Maurice Griffiths 'Good Hope' class ketch. This I believe could be the answer for those who want to build their dream boat in steel, but who don't think that dream boats can be of chine construction.

Designer Robert Hundy, who has extensive experience of steel construction both in Holland and England, has completely redrawn the 'Good Hope' plans for steel construction, and has in the process produced a much more elegant boat. The 'Table Bay' ketch is indeed a very pretty design. Everything is in the right proportions, from the tasteful sheer to the unobtrusive deck-house, from the moderate draft to the compact rig. There is a choice between centre and after cockpit, and 'Table Bay' is also available as a schooner. The design incorporates the use of developed conical surfaces, so that very little plate rolling should be required. And in

98

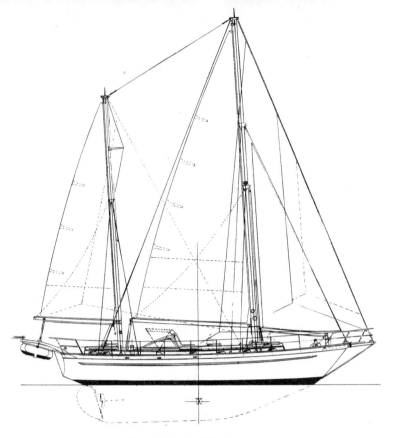

Fig 36 Hundy Table Bay 39.

keeping with the rest of the design, the curvature is moderate
so that the plate can be readily persuaded to shape without
the use of sophisticated machinery. Four mm. steel is used
and this is comparatively easy to bend, while it is still
sufficiently thick to produce fair curves.

For a slightly smaller dream ship with a rounded bilge,
'Tahitiana' could be the answer. Every potential world voyager must know about John Hanna's 'Tahiti' ketch of which
some three thousand have been built since the design first
came off the drawing board more than fifty years ago. They

99

are to be seen sailing all the oceans of the world, economically, safely, and comfortably. Big enough to make a happy home for one or two, small enough to afford, this design is the one I would recommend for the would-be world voyager without a bottomless bank account.

The American designer Weston Farmer was largely instrumental in popularizing 'Tahiti' through publication in the magazine *Modern Mechanics*, of which he was editor at the time. And in 1976 he resolved to bring the old girl back up to date by a complete redesign. Now, the jibe had always been that the 'Tahiti' was comfortable, but oh so slow. So Mr Farmer decided that 'the time has come to bring the old slow "Tahiti" up luffing and square her into the modern breeze' (sic.). He concluded that the reason for her lack of speed was simply lack of sail. And he reached this conclusion after considerable sophisticated research and comparison with other famous voyaging boats such as *Spray*, *Svaap* and *Seabird*. 'Tahiti' at 420 square feet was simply undercanvassed. Answer: 550 square feet of sail.

Mr Farmer reckons that a vessel of her size can be lofted, framed and roughly plated out in a month. And there are plenty more good points. 'Tahitiana' has over 6ft. headroom compared with her predecessor's 5ft. 7½in., and with only a 4in. increase in draft to 4ft. 4in. The headroom makes her much more habitable, and the draft makes her suitable for world voyaging and gunk-holing alike. Mr Farmer has in the process added a couple of inches of freeboard to make a dry boat even drier. A look at 'Tahitiana's' lines will reveal her sea-going qualities and the long straight keel points to good directional stability and comfort, if not to great rapidity in stays. And for a final plus, through a clever design Mr Farmer has managed to obtain a round-bilge effect using multi-chine construction. Conventional straight transverse frames are used, angled at each of three chines. But T-bar longitudinals are also used, and it is around these that the

Fig 37 Farmer Tahitiana.

plates are wrapped. The plates are welded to the longitudinals only, not to the frames, and this allows the plate to 'belly'. And it is this plate-bellying phenomenon that produces a boat of almost round-bilge characteristics.

The plans are available very cheaply from Weston Farmer (see Appendix). The rock-bottom price means that the designer can't enter into correspondence over your construction problems as one could reasonably expect of some of the designers previously discussed. But the plans themselves are detailed, and the construction simple. She should be easy and quick to build.

Just a word about costs. I have tried to give some idea of the cost of plans but I haven't been too specific as prices change all the time. The cost of the plans you like should not be grudged though, for remember it costs just as much to build a bad boat as it does a good one. The material cost of a hull is surprisingly low. And at the time of writing the price per ton is tending to fall rather than rise. This stagnation in steel prices is likely to last because of world over-capacity in steel production. And this can be contrasted with the rapidly escalating resin prices, thus widening the gap between the material cost of a steel hull and that of a GRP hull.

7

Starting to build

The Site

We have had a look at different construction methods and we have selected our set of plans, so there's no excuse now for not getting started. And the first item on the agenda is to find somewhere to build. The requirements for this are simple—a flat, level surface preferably with at least 6 feet of working area around the boat, and a mains electricity supply. Remember to check the electricity for voltage drop as this can cause real problems in the welding. The out-of-the-way places in which boats are usually built are quite often at the end of inadequate cables, so it is best to check with an Avo Meter that the voltage is within 5 per cent of the arc-welding machine's requirements.

Cover is not essential with steel-boat building as it is with most other materials; still, although the steel won't mind the weather, you probably will, so obviously cover is better if there is a choice. The steel itself will not suffer by being exposed to the elements during the time it takes to build. On the contrary, it may even benefit, as the mill scale will be removed by the rusting process, thereby easing the preparation work prior to painting.

A concrete base is ideal for building on, but it must be perfectly level otherwise your boat will probably end up banana-shaped. An area of firm earth is also possible as a building site, and has the advantage that a hole can be dug for the keel, thereby reducing the height of the hull for working on. You will probably be using framed construction, so some form of metal jig will be needed as an anchoring

23 and 24 Building jig using girder sections. (Strip chine construction in progress.)

point for the frames, and this can be used to level up slight undulation. Girder section can be used, as in photos 23 and 24, but a cheaper alternative might be scrap railway lines which can be obtained for around a third of the cost of new tonnage. The lines could subsequently be used as ballast if chopped up into manageable bits. Alternatively, heavy steel plates are sometimes used as a base. While this has got a lot of advantages, the expense of the steel is going to put it beyond the reach of other than professional yards.

Steel Plate

Having organized the site and made sure that no council official or irate neighbour is going to move you on, the next stage is to order the plate. In Great Britain all steel must comply to BS 4360·72, and the coding in other countries is indicated on the table overleaf, which is kindly supplied by Shipyard META in France. The table also indicates the characteristics of the various steels. **Note:** In META's opinion, only the mild steels in the first two columns are suitable for small craft.

English gradings are as follows:
40, 43 or 50 are the grades commonly available and these are measures of Tensile Strength expressed in terms of kgf/mm^2. Alphabetic symbols are added to the numerical, indicating:

    A—No guarantee on yield values
    B—Guarantee on yield values
    C—Guarantee on yield values and impact tests.

Impact-tested plate is not necessary for boat building, but a yield guarantee would be an advantage, so grade 40B would seem the one to buy. META strongly advise to use no other than this ordinary mild steel. And this advice is supported by a research document produced in 1975 by the French Office Technique Pour L'Utilization de L' Acier (OTUA). However, some designers, for example Robert Tucker, specify

TYPES OF STEEL	STEELS IN GENERAL USE				EXAMPLES OF SPECIAL STEELS			
	Mild steel	Mild steel	Semi high-tensile	High-tensile	Special steel	Steel with copper	Low alloy steel	Low alloy steel
					Marinor	Incrasteel 40	Indadur	Cor-ten
Kgfmm^2 (resistance)	33-50	37-45	42-50	52-62	48-60	50-58	48-50	44-49
Great Britain		40B	43B	50A				
U.S.A.		A283grC	A36	A440				
France	A33-1	E24-2(A37)	E26-2(A42)	E36-2(A52)				
Germany	St33-1	St37-2	St42-2					
Belgium	A00	AE22B	AE24B	AE36B				
Italy	Fe33	Fe37-B	Fe42-B	Fe52-B				
Suitability for round-bilge craft	Excellent	Excellent	Difficult	Impossible	Very Difficult	Possible	Very Difficult	Difficult
Suitability for chine craft	Excellent	Excellent	Excellent	Excellent	Excellent	Excellent	Excellent	Excellent
Possibility of welding	No problems	No problems	No problems	No problems	No problems	No problems	No problems	No problems
Practical difficulties in welding	No problems	No problems	Small problems	Tricky	Tricky	Tricky	Small problems	Small problems
Type of welding possible	Arc	Arc	Arc	Gas shielded Arc	Gas shielded Arc	Gas shielded Arc	Gas shielded Arc	Arc
Type of welding recommended	Arc	Arc	Gas shielded Arc	Gas shielded Arc	Gas shielded Arc	Gas shielded Arc	Gas shielded Arc	Gas shielded Arc
Distortion after welding	Medium	Medium	Small	Very small	Very small	Very small	Very small	Small

high-tensile steel (50B with 43A marginally acceptable) and an advantage claimed is that greater fairness in hull plating can be achieved. But most designers and builders to whom I have spoken on the Continent of Europe agree with META, and emphasize that high-tensile steel should not be used as it can have less resistance to fatigue and stresses when welded than does mild steel. It is certainly harder to work than mild steel, especially when cutting is by 'Nibbler' where blade life is reduced by as much as 75 per cent. Welding, too, is more difficult and usually calls for Argon arc.

A special type of semi-high-tensile steel is Cor-Ten, and this has been heralded by many as the answer to the corrosion problem. It is a low-alloy corrosion-resistant steel containing traces of copper. Originally developed for industrial use, Cor-Ten has between five and eight times the resistance to corrosion of ordinary mild steel. It still rusts, but the covering so formed is protective and reduces further wastage. Also the rust is a better basis for paint than that of mild steel, and where the paint covering is damaged the rust doesn't tend to creep under the surrounding good paintwork. However, T. Howard Rogers in his authoritative work *Marine Corrosion* is not enthusiastic about copper-bearing steels in a marine environment. He argues that they can be definitely advantageous in industrial uses, but underwater there is little advantage. There is now evidence to suggest that far from corroding less than mild steel, the copper content in Cor-Ten makes it more prone to electrolysis when immersed in sea water. Tests made in the River Crouch on unprotected mild steel and Cor-Ten plates revealed significantly greater wastage in the Cor-Ten at the end of a year. But the excellent epoxy paint schemes now available have largely eliminated the danger of electrolysis below the waterline anyway, and it is rust creeping under damaged paint on the upper works and inside the hull that causes unsightliness and possible danger. Cor-Ten can do a lot to counteract this.

For most amateurs, however, Cor-Ten is not suitable because it really requires welding by copper-clad continuous-feed electrodes with Argon-arc shielding. Argon-arc machines are expensive at around £1,000 and need to be used indoors, although they can give a better and much quicker weld, and there is some saving on electrodes as against conventional arc. Cor-Ten is harder to cut as well as weld; while a 'Nibbler' blade will probably cut a 40-footer completely out of mild steel before it has to be renewed, the harder Cor-Ten will probably use two or three blades. At around £50 a time that comes expensive.

As a further disadvantage, Cor-Ten sometimes suffers from delivery difficulties and can be over 25 per cent more expensive. I'd go for a good-quality mild steel and spend the money thus saved on thorough grit-blasting and a complete epoxy paint scheme.

With the grade to buy established, what about thickness? This will, of course, be specified in the plans you chose, but it is helpful to know what considerations will have affected the designer in deciding on the specification. Steel is heavy at 490 pounds per cubic foot, but because of its great strength it can be used thinly. However, below 3mm. it becomes very prone to heat distortion and it is consequently difficult to work and to achieve a fair hull. Also it becomes very prone to impact denting. Thicker plate is easier to keep fair, but correspondingly more difficult to bend. Accordingly 7mm. will be about the thickest plate ever encountered on the average yacht, and would be regarded as exceptionally thick except for such as base plates and keels. Beyond this thickness the weight problems become excessive. In practice, 5mm. will be entirely sufficient on most yachts of other than oil-sheikh proportions, and I would not go below 4mm. on the grounds of distortion and corrosion problems. The following table, kindly supplied by Jay Benford, illustrates the comparative weights of different materials:

	Density— Lb./Cu.ft.	Lb./Cu.ft. for thickness suitable for 40ft. sailboat
Aluminium	170	4 to 5
Fibreglass	95 to 115	4 to 6
Wood	21 to 62	4 to 7
Steel	490	7 to 10
Ferro-cement	160 to 200	10 to 13

As can be seen, steel on average comes out second heaviest, after ferro, although these figures are of necessity approximate. To take a specific example, the 40ft. sailboat built in 4mm. steel would be about the same weight as if built in 30mm. teak, both these thicknesses being about right for the job. The steel boat would probably come out lighter if frameless construction was employed.

The price of steel plate varies considerably, so it is best to shop around. For example, in England I found differences of more than £50 a ton when speaking to various yard managers. The more you buy, the cheaper it becomes, so it pays to order the lot in one go. Some designers give you a bill of quantities, but if not, the process of working out quantities helps to familiarize you with every aspect of the plans. The cutting sequence should be worked out to minimize wastage, but some allowance for scrap must be made. I know of one yard that allows 25 per cent scrap in its costings, but that seems excessive to me and a figure of around 20 per cent ought to be easily achievable. Stock sizes of plate are 8 feet by 4 feet and 6 feet by 3 feet (metricated), but other sizes are available and can be specified where appropriate to minimize wastage. However, there are likely to be delivery problems and extra cost involved in the off-standard stuff, so it may be cheaper to weld up on the bench if larger sizes are necessary. But buying long runs of plate does help to minimize the distortion sometimes caused by welded seams. Try to be precise in the amount of plate you order, as excess plate may be hard to dispose of, and running out causes annoying delays as well as increased cost.

It's worth considering buying your plate already shot-blasted and painted with holding primer, as this normally doesn't cost significantly more. In this way you may be able to avoid grit-blasting the inside of the finished hull, although I believe that it is still necessary outside. You can weld through the primer, but obviously it will be burned away locally, so the welds should be wire brushed and strip-primed after each day's work. The holding primer should protect the plate for up to a year under cover or three to four months outside, provided the paint isn't damaged. Grit-blasting on site is an expensive process and a 40-footer could cost about £500. Any grit-blasting is a horrible job, but inside the hull it is particularly unpleasant and, therefore, proportionally more expensive, so the cost should be compared with the extra cost of buying the treated plates. The cost of the blasting operation can be significantly reduced if you do the job yourself, but more of that in Chapter 15.

It is worthwhile ordering all your section steel at the same time as the plate as this increases the tonnage and, therefore, reduces the price. Most sections should be available from steel stockholders in your locality, but British Steel Corporation can supply or advise on stockists if you ask.

Lofting

Having bought your steel, the next stage depends upon the design chosen. The traditional approach is to loft out the plans full size as would be done with a wooden boat. This method has much to commend it in terms of familiarization with the plans and accuracy when the time comes to start building. However, lofting takes a long time and the design may allow alternatives. Bruce Roberts' plans come with full-size paper templates of frames, stem and transom, which eliminate the need for lofting and, therefore, save considerable time. The objection to templates is that they can distort with damp, causing inaccuracies. But provided they are looked after that shouldn't be a real problem and small inaccuracies can be eliminated when the frames are faired in after erection. This is not to condone sloppy work at this stage, because errors of more than ⅛in. or so can be difficult to rectify once the frames are in place and can result in an unfairness in the hull plating which will be very obvious after painting.

Another approach is to work straight from the plans. META plans are drawn with this mind, and use a scale of ten to one to facilitate taking measurements direct from the drawings to the plate or mould floor. The problem with this method is that inaccuracies in extracting measurements will be magnified when taken up to full size. A 1mm. error on the drawings (little more than a pencil line) would be grossed up to 10mm. on the plate, and that is enough to produce unfairness. Nevertheless, META themselves work on this basis, and I have seldom seen such perfect hulls. They take pride in the fact that they never use filler on the plating—nor do they need to. META plans are produced in immense detail (over 50 sheets of drawings) to a fine degree of accuracy, with critical measurements given in figures as well as drawn. And there is the advantage that the drawings are produced by the builders in conjunction with the architect—they have long ago discovered any inaccuracies in the plans because they build boats to them. Additionally, they are able to include useful drawings of tricky features which perhaps the designer may not have foreseen.

The final option is to buy your steel in kit form. At the moment I only know of one firm in England providing this service, P. G. Steelcraft (Marine) Ltd, and their designs suffer from the disadvantage of being only single-chine (although by no means unattractive). But the kit idea is a good one, and I am sure that as steel appeal spreads different kit designs will come on the market and their price may become more attractive. The P. G. Steelcraft kits (imported from De Groot in Holland) fit together by numbers so that no construction plans are needed, just assembly instructions.

The purpose of lofting is to check the measurements given by the designer for accuracy and to provide patterns and template for building. If the plans have been built from many times before, then there is possibly no need to check their accuracy, and only the lofting necessary for pattern production need be undertaken. If the traditional method of complete lofting appears necessary, then it first has to be decided whether to lay out in full scale, half scale or some other fraction. Reducing the scale will, of course, reduce the size of loft floor required, and this may be essential if the boat is a very big one. The transverse sections (Fig. 38) will need to be drawn out full size, and it is helpful if the designer has made these coincide with the frames so that the sections can be used as moulds for frame fabrication. Some longitudinal

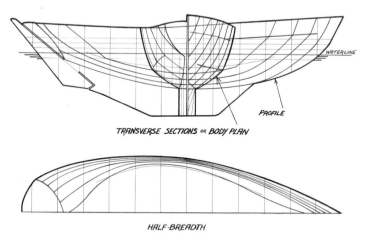

TRANSVERSE SECTIONS or BODY PLAN

HALF-BREADTH

Fig 38 Lines plans.

members such as stem and keel will also need to be drawn full size for fabrication. But the profile and the half-breadth (Fig. 38) can happily be reduced in size to whatever scale is appropriate.

The lofting can be done on paper but this can distort, is easily damaged and inaccuracies can creep in due to its flexibility. Best is to use hardboard or plywood laid out on a level piece of ground (preferably under cover) and painted with white emulsion. Hardboard is cheaper, but I would use 10mm. or 12mm. plywood as this can subsequently be used in fitting out the interior.

You can now take the plans and begin to mark down the lines. Pencil can be used, or ballpoint, the latter avoiding the need for continual sharpening. The first thing to look for is whether the architect projects his table of offsets from a baseline or a given waterline. If it is from a baseline, then the 'bottom' edge of the plywood will serve for this purpose, but if a waterline is used, a straight line will have to be drawn, and this is perhaps best achieved by stretching thin wire across. A batten nailed down will serve equally well. One point to note—obtain the longest measuring tape you can find, at least the length of the boat. Better still get two of them.

The transverse stations must next be drawn in at right angles to the baseline and waterlines. These stations will usefully be at the frames but often designers don't take this trouble and simply take imaginary lines cutting the boat athwartships at appropriate intervals. These station lines serve to locate the table of offsets. This latter is a series of measurements from the baseline or waterline denoting the essential shape of the boat, such as sheer, chine or top and bottom of the keel. The measurements have to be extremely accurate, and the stations have to be drawn precisely at right angles or the resulting errors will be translated into the hull itself.

Now it's necessary to discover whether measurements are

given to the INSIDE of the plating or the OUTSIDE. Inside measurements are obviously necessary for the frames, but outside ones will be necessary for the half breadth etc.

Assuming you are projecting the *profile* first, extract the offsets for each station from the table and mark off from the waterline or baseline. It's then conventional to tap in a nail at these various points leaving half of the nail's length proud of the ply. You then use the nails to fair in the lines. Wooden battens are needed for this job (plastic curtain rail also works), as long and as flexible as possible so that they flex round the nails and can then be used to draw in beautiful fair lines. The battens must be free from knots and must be perfectly straight. A less flexy version might also be useful for the easy sweeps where there are perhaps less stations. With the lines drawn in, they can then be 'eyed up' for fairness: any kinks can be faired out by tacking extra nails in as appropriate. If one or more of the offsets appears to be well adrift, check back to the table. You might have made an error in extracting the figure, but it is entirely possible that the fault lies with the designer himself. This is especially possible if not many boats have been built to the design you have selected. And this is one of the advantages in lofting out in the traditional manner. You have to be very confident that the drawings are fault-free before relying on extracting figures straight from the plans.

As well as the profile, it is conventional to loft out the half breadth, and the body plan. The *half breadth* is a view of half of the boat (port or starboard) seen from below or above. Measurements this time are taken from the centreline, and the baseline of the profile can usefully serve for this to save time and space. As the half breadth is being drawn on top of the profile it is useful to use a different-coloured pen so that the lines can be readily distinguished. When all the lines are drawn in it is a good idea to seal over the top so that they can't be erased or smudged when the loftings are being worked on. Any clear floor sealer or cheap varnish will do for this purpose.

The final job is the *body plan*. This is a view of half the boat seen from either end, but placed side by side. Conventionally the left side of the drawing shows the boat from astern to amidships, and the right-hand side shows it from the bows back to amidships. The lines shown on the drawing represent the various sections of the boat, which hopefully will correspond to the frames. If they do, then the body plan can be used to form templates for frame fabrication. The stern view can also be used as the basis of making up the transom. If this is flat, then no problems should occur in simply taking the measurement from the body plan. However, if, as is preferable, the transom has some curvature built in, this procedure will not work. Chapter 8 looks in detail at transoms, but it is appropriate here to suggest how this curvature may be derived from the body plan. There are a number of mathematical techniques for deducing the increase in size of plate caused by curvature, and these are well described in Chapelle's *Boat Building* which is in fact an excellent reference for all lofting techniques, although primarily aimed at wooden construction. For myself, I prefer the simpler technique of making up a flat template in plywood from the body plan. This template can then be used either before or after plating up the hull to cut out the transom plate. My approach is to cut the plate roughly to shape a bit oversize to allow for the curvature, which is then put in using frames cut to shape from offcuts of steel. The template is then offered up to the embryo transom and the excess plate marked off and subsequently cut. Easy and foolproof.

The profile, half breadth and body plan give all the measurements necessary to start building. It may be useful at this stage to make up measuring sticks for use in the subsequent setting up. These need to be fairly rigid (1 inch by $1\frac{1}{2}$ inches would be all right) and at least two will be needed, one for the sheer or deck edge in profile, and one for the waterline. The centreline and either the sheer or waterline is marked on to the batten at each station. The battens are then used to position the frames precisely.

8

Keels, Ballast and Backbones

The keel is a good place to start welding after all the detailed lofting has been done. It is simple and quick, and provides a sense of achievement at the beginning when it is so badly needed. The keel too, will provide the basis of the backbone if the boat is being built right side up.

The Box-section Keel

By far the most satisfactory type of keel is the *box section* as in the photos 25, 26 and 27. This is usually fabricated out of quite thick plate which then acts as part of the ballast. The base of the keel should be cut out of thick steel (as much as 1 inch) as plenty of margin for corrosion is needed in this area which will be subject to abrasion and to which no paint can be applied. It may be as well to buy this base-plate ready shaped, as 1 inch (25mm.) takes some cutting. The side sections should be at least $\frac{1}{4}$in. and usefully more with the upper restriction on thickness being that caused by the need to bend the plate round towards the forward end of the keel. Plate edges should be bevelled before welding and butted down from above.

Cutting out the plate for the keel can be done either by taking the measurements straight from the loftings or plans, or using a template. But whichever method is chosen, remember to cut the plate sufficiently over length to allow for the curvature towards the keel's forward end. It will be useful when it comes to setting up if the stations are centre-punched on to the keel plate as it is being cut out.

The box-section keel has other advantages apart from

117

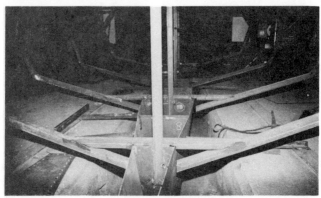

25, 26 and 27 Box-section keels.

simplicity of construction. The keel can be split into compartments which can be used both for ballast and for water and diesel tankage. In this way the ballast can be set as low down as possible and can accordingly be kept to a minimum.

There are a number of possible alternatives for *ballast*. Best is the traditional lead, which at 710lb. per cubic foot is half as heavy again as iron. Accordingly, the centre of gravity will be lower therefore giving improved windward ability in a sailing yacht. Steel punchings are often used as ballast when set in concrete or similar, and this has the advantage of being very cheap. The punchings, which are commonly available from engineering works, can easily be distributed in the box keel, but will take up more space than lead as the tiny spaces between them will reduce their density which in any event is two-thirds that of lead. This means that the centre of gravity will be higher and there will be less room for tankage which could even necessitate the cabin sole having to be raised. Another alternative in larger sailing yachts not expected to perform well to windward is chopped up scrap railway lines, or similar large chunks of metal obtained from a scrap dealer and embedded in concrete.

The price of lead varies considerably from dealer to dealer and can fluctuate on a week-to-week basis by £1 or more per cwt. It's worth shopping around and it's usually worth buying from a scrap dealer despite the fact that a certain amount of impurities can be expected. These will float to the top as dross when the lead is melted for pouring into the keel, and 5 per cent loss can often be expected.

Lead and steel are a long way apart in the galvanic scale so that electrolysis will occur if the two are allowed in contact with each other, to the detriment of the steel. Accordingly the keel is best lined before the lead is fitted. Concrete, fibreglass and bitumastic have all been tried, but the bitumastic would appear to be by far the best as it provides excellent insulation and lasts indefinitely. It doesn't break up or shrink away from the steel like the other two and it has the great advantage of flexibility. If the keel is to be lined in this way, the lead cannot be melted straight in, but has to be fitted in the form of pigs. These pigs will inevitably have slight gaps around them, but these can be kept to the minimum by making the pigs as square as possible. The gaps should be filled with bitumastic melted in around the pigs. If scrap lead is being used, the pigs can be produced by making up a mould out of steel plate. The pigs should be of an easily portable size (say 1 cwt.) and should be of an appropriate length and width so that several of them will exactly fit into the rectangular section formed by the keel. The scrap lead can be melted by a propane blowtorch which could be easily hired from a plant-hire firm. If the inside of the mould is painted with a couple of coats of whitewash this will help to prevent the lead from sticking. The molten lead will have to be puddled to prevent air bubbles being trapped and to help impurities to the surface, and this is traditionally done with green oak sticks as the sap stimulates the trapped air to bubble to the surface. When the mould is full, the dross can be scraped off the surface and the pig allowed to cool. It is best to make up several moulds so that one can be cooling while the next one is being filled. When the mould has cooled sufficiently, in an hour or so, it can be tapped on the base to remove the pig. If the mould tapers slightly towards the bottom, removal will be that much easier.

A useful trick to help in installing the pigs is to insert a steel wire loop so that it solidifies into the molten lead while it is cooling. This will allow the pigs to be lowered down into place much more easily. The wire can be chiselled off after each pig has been installed. Once all the ballast is in position, it should be sealed over the top with a layer of bitumastic. A steel plate can then usefully be welded over the whole lot to stop it all falling out if the yacht should ever be so unfortunate as to invert, and to prevent water getting down between the lead and the steel. If there is a possibility that the ballast may need to be removed, then angle bar can be used to keep it in position and this could easily be chopped out if necessary. If angle bar is used in this way, then the bitumastic would be relied upon to keep bilge water away from the lead. This can cause problems as diesel fuel is a solvent for bitumen, and I can see no real reason against plating over. A simpler alternative to plating may be to concrete over the ballast after retaining it in position with angle.

It can be a good idea to fill only the middle sections of the box keel with ballast initially, leaving the fore and after sections of the box keel empty. In this way the trim can be adjusted precisely when the yacht is afloat by topping up these remaining sections as appropriate. Whatever method you use to cover the ballast, you should ensure that there is a slope towards the stern of the boat, so that any bilge water that does find its way aboard will be collected by the sump. One of the sections in the keel should be reserved as a sump, and remember that this is best deep rather than wide so that bilge water cannot slop out as the boat rolls. An electric submersible bilge pump can then usefully be fitted in the sump together with the suction pipe of a manual stand-by.

As an alternative to making up the pigs, lead is sometimes melted straight into the keel. Provided it is sealed over the top by steel or concrete this should be safe enough but I hesitate to recommend this method because of possible electrolytic problems. It is quite difficult to get the lead into the keel without leaving air bubbles trapped inside. The trick is to do the job slowly melting small bits at a time, and one way to achieve this is by using an iron drain-pipe as a feeder. The pipe is sloped down into the section at as small an angle as possible, and is then heated with the propane blowtorch while small pieces of lead are put in and allowed to melt. The molten lead then trickles down the pipe into the keel where it gradually solidifies.

The Fin and Bilge Keel

Fin and *bilge keels* can be used as ballast formers in exactly the same way as the box-section keel. But in the smaller, perhaps more racy, boats to which fin or bilge keels are commonly fitted, the keels themselves may constitute all or most of the ballast. This is achieved by making them out of heavy plate with a very thick base. One yard that I was shown round in Holland used this technique, constructing their bilge keels of 7mm. plate on the sides and over 30mm. on the base. The design was such that no additional ballast was necessary, but the keels were used as tankage, one for water and the other diesel. The yard designer said that this type of hollow bilge keel configuration gave excellent roll damping properties, and in that respect was appropriate for both sail and power boats. Other advantages of properly designed bilge keels for power boats are that they simplify drying out, and obviate the disturbed water around the propeller that can be caused by the standard keel arrangement.

28   Bilge keel bolted on to a Robert Tucker design. Bolting instead of welding facilitates replacement in the event of damage.

29 Bilge keel: inside strengthening.

Cast Keels

Lead keels should not be bolted to the outside of the boat, as despite the excellent paint schemes now available, serious electrolytic problems will almost certainly occur. Iron or steel ballast keels are sometimes cast for steel boats and bolted on underneath, but I can see little advantage in this method. The expense of casting will almost certainly make the *cast keel* more expensive than scrap lead used in a box keel. Also cast iron and steel have different electrical potentials from mild steel, so there is danger of electrolysis. This would have to be guarded against by putting ample bedding on top of the ballast before it is drawn up. Bitumastic will serve for this purpose, and if put on thick enough it will fill slight unevenness in the cast keel. A further problem of the cast keel is that it has to be secured to the hull by bolting. These bolts have to be extremely strong as they will have to bear all the strain if a yacht goes aground, and there needs to be ample

123

margin for corrosion. The bolts also allow the possibility of water seepage.

There is little justification for using a cast keel. One advantage sometimes put forward is that it can be secured to the hull after building is complete, thereby reducing the height of the hull for working and reducing the weight for moving it around. But a box keel need not be fitted until the rest of the plating is complete, and the ballasting need not be done until she is afloat.

Bolt-on Keels

If you are going to use a bolt-on keel you should specify that the bolt holes are cast in. These are normally made undersize so that they can be subsequently reamed out exactly. The holes must be exactly matched to the boat and this is best done using a template. If this work is done carefully the fitting of the keel can be left to launching day, and this will mean you will only need one day's crane hire. As cranes are commonly hired by the day regardless of the number of lifts this could result in a substantial saving.

The bolts themselves should be substantial. It is a traditional principle of yacht design that each bolt should ideally be capable of supporting the entire keel and it is best not to use stainless ones as these are prone to crevice corrosion and can fracture. Galvanized are best and they should be heavily greased before they are fitted to stop water getting in. White lead around the top and bottom will also help. The bolt heads will have to be recessed at the bottom and provision must be made when casting. Remember to specify that the recess must be big enough to get a ring spanner on to the bolt head. Or have a hexagonal recess cast in and then you could push the bolts up from underneath and tighten the nuts from the inside.

Setting Up the Keel—the First Step

Once the keel is made it can be set up on the building floor as the first step in erecting the hull. However, if space is at a premium it will be appropriate to fabricate the stem and frames as well before setting up begins, so that the mould floor can double as the building floor. In any event this is probably the most appropriate sequence, but I will deal with the setting up of each component part after I have discussed its fabrication in order to avoid too much cross referencing.

The correct setting up of the keel is critical to the shape of the whole boat, and a tendency to sail round corners can often be traced back to errors at this stage. As an aid to accuracy, permanent reference points are needed. And if the boat is being built inside on a level concrete base, this can be achieved by a thin line down the middle of the shop to act as the centreline of the boat, with plumb lines suspended at each of the stations. A centreline scribed on the jig or building floor should complete the necessary reference points, but

30 Setting up the keel.

waterlines and baselines are sometimes marked down the sides of the building, either on the walls, on plates or by wires stretched between uprights. But if you are building your boat outside, marking your reference points may be difficult. One solution is first to construct a steel cradle in which the boat can be built. Reference points can be scribed on or suspended from this structure which can subsequently be used for taking the boat to its launching place.

If the keel is parallel to the waterline, setting up is a simple matter of aligning the keel exactly down the centreline as scribed on the building jig or by a stretched wire. Provided the floor is perfectly level and the keel has been made level, then no further problems should arise. But it is wise to check with the plumb bob that the keel is vertical. However, many sailing boat keels slope down towards the stern which means that the keel has to be set at the correct angle. This should not be a problem, provided the station lines were scribed on the keel at the fabrication stage as suggested earlier in the chapter. The forward end of the keel can be simply raised up, using a hydraulic car trolley jack, until the station line is exactly vertical as proved by the spirit-level or by the vertical plumb bobs. With the keel firmly wedged at this height and perhaps tack welded to the building jig to ensure that it can't move, we can move on to fabricating the stem.

Stems

There are many ways of making a stem, including round bar, tube, flat bar, angle bar or simply plate. All of them have their merits and are used by different designers. Whichever type is specified, the shape will be taken from the loftings first, and the stem will then be set up on the building jig, taking great care to ensure that it is exactly vertical. To achieve this, plumb lines can be set up from the roof or the top bar of your frame along the centreline of the boat. The stem can then be sighted down the lines and set up precisely.

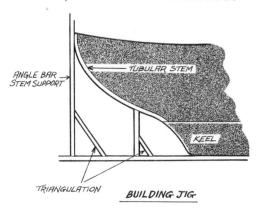

Fig 39 Stem construction.

Assuming the boat is built right side up, the keel will provide the anchoring point for the stem, which will be held up at its forward end by vertical angle bar welded to the building jig. This angle bar will have to be of substantial section and girder may be appropriate on larger boats. A second bar may be necessary at an intermediate point as in Fig. 39. Some advantage in positioning may be derived if the support is attached while on the mould floor; there it can be fitted so as to be precisely vertical. If a horizontal bar is also tacked on parallel to the baseline, then setting up can be done precisely and easily using a triangular support to the stem.

Round bar is commonly used for stems. This is strong, comparatively easily bent without distortion and you can grind it down if necessary. Also it is fairly easy to mate in the plating, as slight cutting inaccuracies can be lost in the join. Round bar gives a fairly fine entry which is appropriate for a sailboat, but perhaps not for a power cruiser where more flare in the bows is generally fashionable. To avoid the stem being excessively heavy it is normal to keep the section below 1in. diameter, and $\frac{3}{4}$in. would be quite common on boats of

31   A simple device for bending bar.

around 40 feet. Much less than this diameter and the bar doesn't have the rigidity to maintain its shape during the plating, so it is just about the minimum even for boats below 30 feet. Round bar can be quite readily bent using a simple device as illustrated in the photograph. The trick is to do the job slowly, making sure that the bar doesn't kink in the direction you are trying to bend it, or twist out of fore and aft alignment (the guides on the bending tool in the photograph are designed to prevent this). Remember that it is much easier to bend the bar some more, than to straighten it after you have gone too far, and that kinks are extremely difficult to correct. For greatest strength the round bar should extend right down into the keel or alternatively down the outside so that it can be fillet-welded for a distance of at least six times its diameter. There will be a loss of strength if the bar is simply butted to the keel.

I can see little purpose in using square section bar, but

there is some merit in rectangular or *flat bar* stems. These are commonly used by a number of designers including Bruce Roberts, but they have the disadvantage that they are difficult to bend to the shape of the stem without distorting in the athwartship plane. It can be done, however, using the bender in the photograph, but it is advisable to keep the bar as narrow as possible. Once bent, the flat bar is extremely strong and the bow plates are easily butted up to it. It may be a bit floppy in the athwartship direction but this can easily be cured by using the second vertical support bar mentioned earlier (Fig. 39) and possibly supporting one or both of them with triangulation.

Tubular stems are also in common use and are favoured by, amongst others, Robert Tucker, in most of his designs for amateur building. The principal advantage of this method is that, weight for weight, tube has the greatest strength of any of the sections we have looked at. It will maintain its shape best in both the fore-and-aft and the athwartship planes, and is perhaps also the most forgiving when it comes to fitting in the bow plates. Against this is the fact that tube is comparatively difficult to bend without kinking, although the hire of a

32 Tubular stem on a Robert Tucker design.

pipe bender should solve this problem, and in any event it's no harder than flat bar. Perhaps more serious is the fact that unseen corrosion can take place on the inside of the pipe, and for this reason it is not acceptable to Lloyd's amongst other construction authorities. Such corrosion shouldn't be a serious problem if all access of water is prevented by blocking off each end of the tube, and if the tube is galvanized before fitting. The galvanizing will cause problems when welding up the bow plates, so the outside galvanizing must be ground off where the welds will come, before plating begins.

Problems can arise in joining the tube to the keel. A straight join can cause a sharp loss in strength. An angle join will be better but may be difficult to arrange. Some advantage may be gained by slicing off half of the bottom of the tube and joining it to the keel as in Fig. 40. Alternatively the whole tube can be taken to the bottom of the keel and the gap between tube and keel filled in with fillet welds.

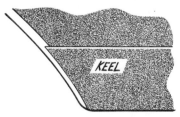

Fig 40 Joining the keel to the stem.

The tube will probably be at least 2 inches in diameter, but there is some sense in checking the size of pipe bender available before finally deciding. The pipe should be of high tensile steel and drawn, not welded, as the welded pipe will have tensions locked in it which are best avoided. Tube will give a much blunter entry than the previous methods looked at, depending on its diameter. This is likely to meet with approval in power boats as a greater flare in the bows can be achieved, but it may not be so appropriate in sailboats,

33 Tapered semi-conical section for stem of a *Joshua*-class boat,
at META's yard.

although the fine entry is really important only in racing
boats, and even then it is below the waterline that matters
most.

The final option is the *plated* stem. Here the bow plates are
run together and welded to each other with no supporting
stem bar. Commonly used in frameless construction, this
calls for extreme accuracy in the plating and it is doubtful if it
will go right at the first offering. However, it has the merit of
being very simple, and by virtue of the angular meeting of the
plates, amply strong in boats below about 40 feet. Where
there is excessive flare, plating up without a stem bar could
be extremely difficult. But in this case it is common practice
to have a tapered semi-conical section made up by sub-
contract, as in photo 33, showing a *Joshua*-class boat building
at META's yard in France. Whatever the bow shape, the
lack of a stem bar seems to me to make life more difficult as
there is nothing to hang the bow plates on to. It would appear
to be most viable if the boat is being built upside down so that

the plates fall naturally together. One possibility is to have a bar only behind the flare, and especially where it starts to increase rapidly towards deck level if a clipper bow effect is being sought. There would appear to be little advantage in this other than marginal weight saving. And there is the additional problem of how to fair the bar into the plated stem without it being very noticeable.

With regard to repairs, the plated stem will be the easiest of the lot, especially if there is plenty of flare so that you can get in behind to cut and bend. The tube will be the most difficult as collision damage will almost certainly cause a kink which will be almost impossible to straighten. It will probably have to be cut out, and a new section welded in. Round bar will be a bit easier to straighten, but compared with other parts of the hull any form of stem is hard to repair.

The choice for amateurs? For me flat bar is the best as it is strong, and can easily be bent using the home-made jigs illustrated in photographs 31 and 34.

34 Home-made jig for bending flat bar.

Transoms

It is seldom that the box keel extends right to the transom. Normally the two will be joined by a longitudinal which will carry the skeg if it is a fin-and-skeg design, or allow for an inboard rudder. The longitudinal will have to be firmly supported at its after end by a vertical from the building jig, as it will have to carry its share of the plating and support the transom.

The longitudinal can be made up out of any of the sections that we looked at for the stem, but my preference is for flat bar. This is because flat bar will fall naturally to the small amount of curvature normally required, rigidity being achieved by ensuring that the vertical support from the jig is strongly secured, particularly in the fore-and-aft direction. As an additional advantage, the flat bar can be welded easily and strongly to the keel. The flat bar should be kept fairly narrow, or it will be difficult to avoid a flat appearance at the bottom of the transom, which looks unsightly unless it's below the waterline. Better is to use plate about 6 inches wide, and a bit thicker than the skin plating, say $\frac{1}{4}$in. (If the strip chine technique [see p. 81] is being used, some of that plating will be ideal.) Before fitting, the after end of this plate can be gradually shaped to the curve of the transom, by heating and thumping on an anvil.

Once this longitudinal is fitted, the transom can be cut out and positioned, perhaps supported by another vertical from the jig. If you are building on steel moulds, there is some merit in cutting out the transom slightly oversize so that you can see how the plates run aft. And they will always run slightly differently because of the tensions set up in the steel when it was rolled. The transom can then be ground away as appropriate. An alternative is to fit a hardboard mock-up, using that subsequently to cut out the steel transom exactly to suit the plate run. On framed construction (or frameless with bulkheads as formers), the transom is best cut to shape from the plans and welded up strongly to the longitudinal straight away.

Transoms are often curved. This gives greater strength, looks attractive and is not difficult to achieve. A curvature of about 1:8 would be reasonable, and the plate would flex to that without need of rolling. Some stiffening will be necessary to hold the transom shape prior to plating, and this is perhaps most easily achieved by cutting stiffeners out of scrap plate. Round bar is sometimes used to edge the transom and this all adds to the strength. It can also improve the appearance, as rounded edges will be achieved, and as an additional bonus the paint will wear better at the corners. Plating up is also made easier as the round bar will cope with slight inaccuracies in cutting out the stern plates. The disadvantages are the extra weight and the extra demand on your time.

Portholes are good to have in the transom if the boat has an after cabin. Being able to watch the wake stream out astern is all part of the luxury of this fine design feature, and the extra light will also be welcome. For both safety and appearance, the portholes should be recessed and this also gets over the problem of curving glass to fit the curvature in the plate. Fitting these portholes (without the glass) is something that can usefully be done before erecting the transom. Remember to allow for the transom slope when making the surrounds so that the window is not only flat but vertical as well.

A rectangular porthole is the easiest to make but looks terrible. Rounding the corners gives an immediate improvement in appearance and is not too difficult. A reasonable approach is to bend two pieces of $\frac{1}{8}$in. plate into a U shape by beating on the anvil. The two U shapes can then be welded together, doing the job very slowly to prevent distortion. The size of the porthole largely depends on personal preference, but the width of the surround depends on the slope of the transom. Assuming a transom that slopes aft, the bottom of the porthole surround can usefully be inset about 1½ inches and the top will be that bit more depending how much slope there is from the vertical. Once this steel hoop has been made, it can be offered up to the transom and marked round the edge. A hole can be cut out with the 'Nibbler' and the hoop pushed through and juggled until it is horizontal. It can then be tack welded on the inside and the protruding part of the hoop cut away with the angle-grinder. The whole thing can then be welded solid and will act as part of the transom stiffening.

Skegs

Skegs are normally fitted to sailboats with fin keels, and on most power boats. They can give somewhere to hang the rudder and often provide support for the propeller tube. Most of all, they give considerable directional stability which would otherwise have to be achieved by an overlarge rudder.

35 Bolted-on skeg, providing support for the rudder.

About a third of a rudder's area can be converted to a fixed skeg without loss of rudder efficiency and with a great gain in stability. The skeg is commonly made out of thick plate on power boats and on some small bilge-keel sailboats. To give greater resistance against bending sideways on bigger power boats and most sailboats the skeg will be made up hollow out of thinner plating. Because of the virtual impossibility of painting inside it will often be filled with concrete. The skeg needs to be very strongly attached to the hull as considerable strain may be imposed upon it if the boat grounds. This probably won't be achieved by simply butt welding the skeg to the stern longitudinal, so it's better to cut out the shape of the top of the skeg in the longitudinal plate and protrude the skeg through into the inside of the boat. It can then be welded inside and out and a good strong joint can be achieved. The fore part of the skeg can be made out of round bar, tube or plate in the same way as stems. If round bar is used, this can be extended up into the boat and used to strengthen the joint. There is no real need to fit the skeg at this stage and it can well be left till nearer the end of the hull construction, at which time the stern longitudinal will be strengthened by the hull plating.

9

Frames, Bulkheads and Beams

If frames are to be used (see Chapter 5 for alternatives), the choice of systems is vast. The traditional approach uses transverse web frames at between roughly 15in. and 24in. centres depending on the size of the boat. These frames are often supported by plated floors at some or all of the centres. In conjunction with the system, longitudinal framing is sometimes employed where great strength is required or to reduce the risk of denting where thin plates or widely spaced frames have been used. The transversal method is the one assumed by Lloyd's in their scantling rules, although it is largely a legacy from the traditional structural thinking of wooden boats. It works for both round-bilge and chine construction, and in many instances it's the best way to do the job—but not always.

Longitudinal Framing
Longitudinal framing was first applied to big steel ships, the reason being that they are relatively weak in a fore-and-aft direction. This is not the case in small boats where plating of 5mm. or more can provide ample strength without any framing at all. The frames are just there to stop denting by keeping the size of unsupported panel as small as possible. Provided this objective is achieved it doesn't matter whether frames go athwartships or fore-and-aft, or both.

Longitudinal framing can make for easy building, whereas transverse frames can easily lead to plate distortion and wobbly topsides; longitudinals don't seem to be as prone to this problem. And such distortion as does occur is less offensive to the eye on the horizontal as opposed to the vertical plane. In addition, transverse frames take a relatively long time to fabricate, whereas longitudinals can simply be wrapped round previously erected bulkheads with perhaps one or two widely spaced transverse frames. There should be little need for prior forming provided there isn't excessive flare at the bows or curvature at the stern, and provided the frame scantling is chosen appropriately. One inch by one inch angle, ⅛in. thick, would probably be suitable on most boats up to around 40 feet as it can be easily bent. But avoid a section with a deep inboard web as this would be difficult to bend.

The main disadvantage of the longitudinal system is that the frames can act as water traps. But there are a number of solutions to this problem. If the frames are set at an angle towards the bottom of the boat, not only does this prevent water collecting, but bending round the hull is made easier (Fig. 41). Painting behind angle shaped in this fashion would be impossible, so flat bar is necessitated by this approach. Limber holes drilled at appropriate intervals are another

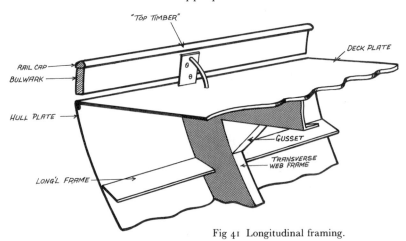

Fig 41 Longitudinal framing.

possibility, but they tend to get blocked and you can't see if they are doing their job behind ceilings. In the cargo holds of large vessels it is common practice to make a sloping fillet of cement in the angle formed by the longitudinal. And I can see every reason for using the same technique in the boats we are talking about.

The only other problem with the longitudinal system is the need to recess the bar into the transverse frames and/or bulkheads. But this is nothing compared to the time that can be saved. Fig. 41 shows a hull section with a longitudinal frame recessed into a main transverse frame more strongly and more easily than with angle or T bar.

Framed or Frameless

In Chapter 5 we looked at the advantages of frameless construction and saw that one can either use a mould or build on a bulkhead. With either approach, frames are commonly added after the hull is complete in order to support the plating. Working this way round reduces the likelihood of plate distortion at the frames and can speed up the whole job. This approach is the one used by England's Robert Tucker in most of his designs and is common on the Continent of Europe as well; META of France for example use it in the production of their 'Defer'.

Surprisingly most designs I have come across that call for retrospective framing in this way use a transversal system. As the chines provide longitudinal strengthening it would seem logical to continue this on the topside plating by using fore-and-aft frames, especially as they are normally easier to fit than transverse ones which require greater forming. De Groot use longitudinal framing for their hulls and kits which are very popular in Holland.

Where transverse frames are employed, the section can be used straight if flat bar fillets are welded in to fill the gap between the frame and the hull. This doesn't appeal to me, though, as it seems rather amateurish, and the plating isn't supported by the whole frame.

Frame Sections

The choice is between angle bar, T bar or flat bar, with angle being the conventional section approved by Lloyd's.

Angle bar has a number of advantages. It is readily available from all steel stockists in all sizes usually necessary for boat construction, and has immense strength when welded to the hull plating so as to form a channel. It also has enough strength to keep fairly rigid longitudinally at the framing stage, unlike flat bar which will be quite floppy.

However, *Flat* bar, which is also easily available, is simpler to bend with amateur equipment and has the advantage that both sides are accessible for welding. It can be difficult to get the rod in to weld behind angle in some parts of the hull. Flat bar also saves weight and is easier to maintain than angle

36   Set of flat bar frames for *Joshua* class.

which creates a rust-trapping 'nook'. And as an additional bonus it is simpler to attach wooden battens to flat bar when the time comes for fitting out (fitting the cladding straight on to the angle is a longer and more difficult process).

T bar is a good choice where great strength is required. It bends more readily without distortion than either angle or flat bar, and welding accessibility is not a problem as with angle. However, it is sometimes difficult to obtain, and it often costs slightly more than other sections.

Frame Spacing

The spacing of frames will be decided by a combination of factors, including plate thickness, size of boat and the use to which she will be put. The thinner the plate and the more rugged the use, the greater the need for closely spaced frames. But in most small yachts frames serve the principal purpose of preventing dents in the plates, rather than of strengthening the structure. Because of this there is a bit more choice when it comes to frame spacing than for example in a wooden boat which depends upon its frames to hold all the separate planks together. Accordingly, frames can be positioned to suit building convenience up to the maximum gap which will give sufficient support against denting. There is no need to have them all the same distance apart and it is common to have closer spacing at the ends where more shaping is required. This simplifies plating and makes for a fairer hull. A clever designer will also have regard to the interior layout when specifying frame intervals. Bulkheads and furniture are most conveniently fastened to frames so the spacing should be made with this in mind. Twenty inches is often appropriate as four times this amount gives a 6ft. 6in. berth, and is also an appropriate width for a hanging locker.

Flat bar would be my choice, and it is commonly used by amateurs and professionals alike. For example, Bruce Roberts uses it in all his designs for amateur construction, and META of France use it for their immensely strong range of round-bilge voyaging yachts.

Frame Forming

Sophisticated yards have sophisticated frame-forming machinery but I doubt many readers will be in that league. No matter, because simple devices can achieve the same ends with not so much more time. Perhaps the best is the simple frame bender explained by the photograph 31.

Provided the section is bent gradually along its entire length and continually checked for distortion, no problems should be experienced in cold-forming metal of the dimensions commonly used for framing.

An alternative technique for bending angle so that a flat is presented to the plating (not the strongest form) is to lay the bar on a flat surface and hammer along the vertical edge. The trick is to hit the bar hard in the middle, and this action will tend to bend it up at either end. Then get an assistant to hold one end so that part of the bar is again flat on the ground. Bash this bit hard in the middle and again the bar will bend in the required direction. Then simply continue with this process sighting along the bar for flat spots and eliminating them with a hefty thump. Make sure the bar is perfectly level though, before you hit, or it will be hard on your assistant's hands! The technique will also work with flat bar. It is easily possible to achieve a camber of an inch in a foot in this way.

Heavy sections, such as those used under the mast, will not be so easily formed and will require other techniques. One way out is to have this small amount of work done by a specialist, but even that doesn't always prove successful. I once had some deck beams made by a firm of ship repairers and the job was so badly done that I had to scrap several and cold-form new ones myself. A successful alternative to cold-forming is to cut the frames out of solid plate. This is not so time-consuming as it might sound, nor as wasteful. It can often be quicker to cut out a frame than to attempt to bend it up without the proper equipment, and cutting out one frame can form one edge of the next. If greater strength is required than is provided by the flat plate, then flat bar can be welded on at right angles. Another old-fashioned alternative is to cut the standing web of the angle bar at frequent intervals, thereby allowing the bar to bend. The cuts are welded up again, while ensuring that there is sufficient bend to allow for the pull of the welding. This is a long tedious process, but it may be the only way if very heavy section is required. Better in my view not to have such sections in the design, and if extra strength is required at the mast, to use a bulkhead or a pillar.

Bulkheads and Pillars

I am in favour of steel bulkheads having had a serious fire contained by one, while in the uncomfortable position of being only a few miles off the Lizard Point in Cornwall with an onshore Force 7. But some people don't like them, arguing that they add unnecessarily to weight and split up the accommodation in an inconvenient way. I respect the point, but believe that the advantages of fire and flood protection, as well as structural considerations, handsomely outweigh these problems which can, I believe, be solved by sound design. Our own boat has two such bulkheads; the forward one sections off the heads and forepeak (no bad thing) and supports the foremast, while the after bulkhead segregates the sea cabin from the civilized accommodation, and there is access through both bulkheads via watertight doors. Still, the steel used in our bulkheads is much too thick, 4·75mm. ($\frac{3}{16}$in.) whereas 3mm. would have been quite adequate, and the thick plate has added unnecessarily to weight. In fact, quite thin plating can be used successfully (I have seen $\frac{1}{16}$in.) provided it is adequately supported. Nor is copious unsightly framing necessary with clever design. The watertight door coamings will give strength, and steel framework for furniture can also be designed to give support. More subtly, engine-room partitioning, tankage or companionways can often be arranged in such a way as to eliminate the need for specifically stiffening the bulkhead.

Partial steel bulkheads extending from the sides inwards are common on many small boats, particularly those employing frameless construction. While obviously not giving any fire or flood prevention advantages, these can provide considerable structural support. They can be used as mast supports and to section off the forepeak, or perhaps to form the basis of a hanging locker. Situated aft they can be used as part of the engine compartment, or as support for a centre cockpit. Normally, they will extend in from the hull plating for the full extent of the side decks, assuming a coach roof is fitted, and act as a sort of deep frame.

Plywood bulkheads can be used as an alternative and if well bolted to steel frames they can give some structural support. Three-quarter-inch ply, however, is probably the thinnest to serve for this function and this offers no weight saving on $\frac{1}{16}$in. steel. The wood can give a more attractive finish, but large areas of exposed plywood are no more pleasing than a painted steel bulkhead. And in any event the steel can be attractively disguised by cladding with cork tiles. But it must be admitted that plywood does have useful insulation properties (heat and sound) which the steel plate won't possess to the same degree.

But watertight bulkheads do give rise to a number of problems. First, to be watertight they must obviously be welded all round and ideally on both sides. Such excessive welding will not be indulged in at other frames on the grounds that considerable shrinkage and distortion must occur with the more serious possibility of stress raisers being created. One way out of these problems is to skip-weld as normal at the bulkheads and gain the watertightness with fibreglass and resin or one of the epoxy fillers. This would give problems only if you had fire and flood at the same time—an unlikely occurrence in a steel boat. Along the same lines is the difficulty of making watertight the inevitable propeller shaft and cable apertures. The propeller shaft will clearly need glands but the cables can be run high and watertightness is probably not vital right up to deck height. The other serious difficulty is the fabrication of the watertight doors. A steel version will be very heavy, an alloy one expensive. Our forward door is steel and has so far only claimed one fingernail. We understand it, but it has been known to attack strangers. We vetoed steel for our after door as this is frequently used at sea. I'd have liked an alloy version but had no means of welding one up and so had to resort to the ubiquitous plywood. Asbestos (yes the blue sort!) sandwiched between plywood provides a measure of fire resistance, and rubber sealing strips have, I hope, given an element of watertightness.

Pillars are an alternative to bulkheads where support is needed for a broad expanse of deck, or for a mast or winch. Such pillars have to be cleverly designed into the accommo-dation plan as no owner will want a pillar coming for example straight down through his double bunk (one well known plastic design has exactly this). Such stupidities should never occur, indeed the pillars should be turned to advantage inside by using them as hand holds, furniture supports, tank feeder pipes or even, as I saw on one William Garden design (wood), as the posts of a four-poster bunk!

Frame Fabrication
Accuracy at this stage is essential in order to avoid a hull which looks like a ploughed field. Just as a reminder, check whether measurements are given to the outside or the inside of the plating—the inside is, of course, necessary for frame fabrication. The precise procedure for starting will depend

upon whether the hull has been fully lofted, or templates or scale drawings are being used (see Chapter 7).

If *Lofting* has already been done, the body-plan can provide the shape for frame fabrication provided the sections correspond to the frame intervals (oh considerate designer!). If not, then critical points will have to be measured off from the lofted half breadth and hull profile, as at the frame position. These points, such as top and bottom of keel, chine, waterline, sheer, deck-edge, etc., can usefully be transferred from the loftings to the fabrication floor by means of the rigid sticks mentioned in Chapter 7. This floor, best made out of plate, can usefully be scribed and centre-punched permanently with the appropriate centreline and base or waterline, and these will act as reference points for transferring the loftings.

Where *templates* are provided by the designer, it is still best to centre-punch the shape of the frames on to a plate fabrication floor. This is because the templates will quickly become damaged with the constant offering up of frames, and in any event they can distort through damp by as much as half an inch in a twenty-foot run.

Dimensions shown on the plans are sometimes used direct where the designer's figures have been proved by previous constructions to be sufficiently accurate, and where the drawings provide sufficient detail (for example META in France). But with this method, too, it's as well to scribe out and centre-punch the frame shapes on to a steel fabrication plate upon which construction can proceed direct.

When it comes to cutting the steel for the frames, I find it best to cut fractionally over-length then offer up the piece to its precise spot on the fabrication plate, and finally mark and cut exactly to size. In my view, the gas cutting torch has no place in this operation because of distortion. Gilbert Klingel in his otherwise most useful book *Boat Building with Steel* goes to great lengths to describe how to minimize and correct distortion due to gas cutting, whereas none of it is required if the metal is cut by cutting disc in the angle-grinder. Simple, and in many ways more accurate and quick. The same issue will arise when it comes to plating, but more of that in the next chapter.

Some beginners tend to join the bits of frame with long overlaps. This practice which probably stems from wood construction, looks amateurish and stops the frame lying flat. It also adds unnecessarily to weight and is probably weaker than a proper butt joint, especially as rust can form between the mated surfaces. The best procedure is to cut the two edges to be joined so that they precisely match, and then bevel them in order to ensure complete penetration.

Great care should be taken not to pull the frames out of alignment during welding. A tiny movement at the weld can result in several inches' throw several feet away. So to ensure against this, it is best to pay particular attention to aligning the joint and to the welding sequence. A tack in the middle of the butt shouldn't cause any pull either way, so this is the best place to start. It can then be useful to triangulate across the join by tacking on scrap angle. If the angle is tacked on one side only, it will be easy to knock against the tacks to break the bar away. This method is probably better than tacking to the fabrication plate where it may be harder to break the tacks loose. If triangulation is used to lock the frame in position, it is still essential to take care over the welding sequence, or unwanted stresses can be built into the bar to cause distortion when the triangulation is released. Best is to tack progressively outwards from the centre tack on the side of the bar without the bevel. The tacks can usefully be made with as low an amperage as possible so as to apply the minimum of heat. With the frame now solidly joined together, the bevelled edges can be pass-welded from the centre outwards, welding as quickly as possible in both directions one after the other so as to equalize the pull. The tacked side can then be welded in like fashion. As this procedure involves turning over the frames, it is perhaps useful to tack all the joints at one go, so that each step can be done to all the joints at the same time. This has the additional advantage of minimizing distortion by creating a strong hoop effect. For the pass-welding as well as the tacking, I prefer to use small rods (maximum 12 s.w.g.) as this enables heat input and consequent distortion to be kept to a minimum. The same goes for plating later on.

Quite often plated *floors* are specified in the design, and these can be welded into the frame hoop to increase its strength. They are commonly included towards the ends of the boat, where strength isn't provided by the keel. The compartments thereby created can serve for a number of purposes such as tankage, chain locker or even a lockable duty-free compartment as on our boat.

Ideally, the floors should be the same thickness as the frames in order to avoid a weak point at the joint. And the tops of the floors can usefully be arranged so as to be all the same height. This simplifies fitting out, but the relatively complex measurements required may not be warranted, as levelling off with angle bar after the hull is complete is often satisfactory. Indeed, the plated floors will need a flat top anyway if floorboards are to be fitted, and angle bar can be used for this purpose, and for that of levelling. Bar welded at a right angle to the top of the floor in this way will also impart extra strength to the frame hoop.

Sometimes *gussets* are specified in the absence of complete floors (see Fig. 42). These are seldom really necessary strengthwise as properly joined bar of the appropriate size should be amply sufficient. Gussets are probably a hangover from wooden construction days and those more used to wooden design often forget that steel boat frames serve a different purpose from those in a wooden boat. Wooden frames have to hold a number of small planks together,

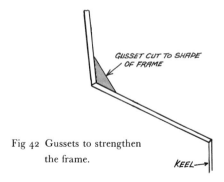

GUSSET CUT TO SHAPE
OF FRAME

Fig 42 Gussets to strengthen
the frame.

KEEL→

whereas a steel skin has sufficient strength in itself. If gussets
are to be used, perhaps for local strengthening, then they
should be cut to the shape of the frame as in the diagram, and
butted rather than overlapped. They can interfere with the
fitting out process and are in my view only warranted at high
stress points such as, for example, at the mast.

Deck beams should be added at the framing stage, as this
completes the hoop. I am strongly in favour of flush decks for
reasons discussed elsewhere (p. 16), and they also have the
merit that they considerably simplify making the beams. The
beams themselves will be cambered as this gives the advantage of rapid water drainaway, extra headroom and a more
pleasing appearance. And in a sailing boat camber makes it
easier to walk along the weather deck. Excessive camber,
however, like extremes of anything on a boat, does not look
right and 1 in. in 1 ft. is about the most that is acceptable to the
eye. A butt joint to the frames should be amply strong, but
sometimes brackets are specified by the designer. These
brackets are seldom really necessary and from personal
experience on our own boat I know that they make life harder
at the fitting out stage. Again, they are probably a hangover
from wooden construction thinking. One design I know
compromises by having brackets at every other frame, but

this seems to me to be the worst of both worlds. Only a little time is saved at the fabrication stage and the weight reduction is minimal, and fitting out is more difficult. In our boat I made them into a feature by sloping the cladding from the ship's side to the deckhead, using battens screwed to the brackets as support. With intermediate brackets missing, the support interval would have been too great.

Where a *coach roof* is included in the design, the framework for it can be fabricated at the hull framing stage and incorporated into the hoop. But it may sometimes be better to beam right across as though the boat were a flush decker and make up the coach roof later. In this way the precision job of frame formation can be achieved without the added complexity of the coach roof's extra angles. The coach roof can then be fabricated at workshop floor level and subsequently fitted after the hull is rigidly welded up. This means that the height of the roof can be slightly adjusted up or down if it appears advantageous for headroom or appearance after the hull is complete. Cutting out the full-width beams in order to fit the coach roof should be a quick job and it can be done without distortion if the angle-grinder is used. The piece cut out will then serve as the coach roof beam. This method has specific advantages where building headroom is limited.

Erecting the Frame Hoops

With the frame hoops all fabricated it is now time to return to the building floor. If, as has been suggested, you have used flat bar, your frames will be a bit floppy, and it is a good idea to tack-weld an angle bar vertically to the hoop, and perhaps another horizontally. If these bars are attached precisely at the centreline and at the waterline, then they can be of considerable assistance in the setting up. With the frame precisely positioned on the centreline you can use the spirit-level clamped to the support bars to check that the hoop is both vertically and horizontally aligned. The plumb bobs can also help, and as a final check you can take a tape and measure from a fixed point on the stem to the sheer point on both sides of the frame hoop. If the measurement isn't exactly the same, you must adjust, or your boat will turn out banana-shaped. Once the middle frame and perhaps one or two more have been set up precisely, then the others can be set up by measurement from their nearest neighbours, with a simple plumb bob check on the centreline supports to ensure that they are vertical.

After each frame is erected it will have to be secured in position by angle bar up from the jig, or out from the sides of the building, or cradle. This won't ensure complete rigidity, which will only start to be introduced when some longitudinals are added. If none of these is included in the design then it will probably be necessary to tack angle bar fore-and-aft along the inside of the frames. Tacked on one side only, these bars should provide sufficient longitudinal strength during plating, and they will be easily removable afterwards by knocking against the tacks. However, in my view, some form of integral longitudinals are necessary in framed construction and at the very least, chine bars and sheer bars should be fitted.

The advantages of chine *stringers* of various section were looked at in Chapter 5 on steel construction systems and the discussion of various stem bar types in Chapter 8 is also relevant here. While there is no purpose in renewing the discussion, I would reiterate my preference for round bar. Sheer stringers are also a good idea in my view in that they provide additional longitudinal support, can produce a neat deck-edge and give a line against which to butt the plating. In general the same arguments with regard to sections apply to the sheer stringer as to the chine stringer. But I can see a lot of advantage in using fairly large diameter tube notched only half-way into the frames so that the other half stands proud. This then acts as a very neat and very simple rubbing strake which can look most attractive if painted a contrasting colour. Other ideas for finishing off the deck-edge appear in the next chapter on plating, but I believe this to be as good as any.

If other longitudinal stringers are used, then there is a choice between notching-in or cutting the bar to fit between the frames. The former method is probably stronger, but the latter simpler and quicker. And as the longitudinals are really only there to stop denting, and to help in keeping the hull fair during construction, it is the method I would recommend. With the short lengths of bar, no problems should arise in bending the steel to the fore-and-aft curve of the boat. But this might be a problem with the chine and sheer stringers, and a pipe bender will be of considerable assistance. A fair curve in these stringers is essential for the look of the boat, so every care should be taken at this stage. Accurate notching-in will be critical to achieving this fair curve, and it is conventional to make-up a 'notch template' for this purpose. The notch is best cut with the cutting disc on the angle-grinder so as to avoid the heat of the cutting torch.

The final job before plating is to make sure that all the frames are fair by sighting down then using the fairing batten.

10

Plating

The Best Approach

Plating is make or break time. So a few words on the overall approach to the job might be useful before I go into the detail. The art is to prevent too great a temperature rise in any part of the structure, as excessive heat causes the plates to shrink on subsequent cooling and distort. Some distortion is almost inevitable, but a proper welding sequence can keep it to a minimum.

First you must mark out the plates. It is normal to mark out and fit one pair of plates (port and starboard) at a time, starting from the middle of the ship and working towards either end. You should only lightly tack the plates in position until all the framework is covered, and then the seams can all be tack-welded. It is important to even up the stresses of tacking, by working on first one side of the boat and then the other, and by working progressively from the middle towards either end. I prefer to see the tacking on the inside of the hull so that the outside seams can be welded free from interference by slag-producing tacks. But this is not always easy to arrange. In any event, the tacks should be widely spaced to start with, and then the gaps should be gradually reduced to about 3 inches by working progressively around the boat in the manner already described. This done, you can fully weld the seams on the outside, taking care to use the back-stepping technique (p. 71), and to keep temperature rise to a minimum. You can then complete the welding of the inside seams. But before welding to the frames it is best to fair the hull plating using one of the techniques described later.

However, the process of welding to the frames can in itself cause some distortion. So the frame welding must also be done with great care, working progressively as before, and keeping the length of run to a minimum.

Marking Out

As with every other stage there is more than one way of marking out. I know of only a handful of professional yards that can develop plates straight off the lines plan, so this highly skilled method is not really open to us. The alternatives are templating or offering the plates up to the framing and marking out direct, both these ways being used by yards of my acquaintance. Gilbert Klingel in *Boat Building with Steel* comes down heavily in favour of templating, believing the alternative to be unprofessional and an indicator of shoddy work. But many highly reputable yards to whom I have spoken prefer to mark out direct, saying that this can lead to greater rather than less precision. So the answer must be for you to choose the method you find easiest. For myself, I have found it best to plate up direct, but my experience has been with boats of comparatively simple shape and developed plates. Once you start getting into compound curvature, I can well believe that templating would be a must.

If you chose to take *templates* first, hardboard is as good as anything to use, being cheap and having similar bending characteristics to steel. Three-millimetre should be sufficient. Some yards prefer stiff cardboard or even paper, but this could lead to imprecision around the edges. Klingel recommends pasting up strips of hardboard into the required shape, but this seems to me to be unnecessarily messy for a minimal saving in cost.

My approach is to cut the plate roughly to shape from measurements, making sure that it is several inches oversize. I then offer it up to the framing and mark out the exact shape using french chalk (felt tip pens also work). The plate then comes down and is cut to the chalk lines (although in some cases such as deck-edges, the excess can be cut off *in situ*). I find this method to be both quick and accurate, the only disadvantages being the bit of extra cutting and the fact that the plate has to be offered up twice. The first problem is offset by the fact that the hardboard doesn't have to be cut (or bought!), and the extra plate manoeuvring shouldn't matter if the job is organized properly.

Cutting and Edge Preparation

We had a look at alternative ways of cutting in Chapter 3, but I repeat my dislike of gas for this purpose. Assuming that the 'Nibbler' or cutting discs are being used, the cut edges will be smooth and straight, but unless welding is by Argon arc, it is usually best to bevel the edges as well, before welding begins. Just a few boats are produced with overlapping seams and those from META are an example (see photo 37).

37 Hull made with overlapping seams, at META, France.
(Note hoops for turning hull.)

The result can be attractive if the seams are made to follow the sheer, and it is undoubtedly very strong. With an overlap of an inch or so, the inside and outside welds are spread, thereby reducing stress. And the stronger fillet-weld form is required. Another advantage is the fact that the double thickness of plate acts almost as a longitudinal stringer. But against all this is the difficulty of keeping the seam following the shear, and the (slight) risk of corrosion between the overlapped plates.

A bevel helps ensure that proper penetration is achieved, and is best done on the outboard side of the plate. The outside weld can then be ground smooth and the inside double weld left proud. This will make for the best appearance and should ensure that the seams are watertight. (Although 3mm. plate is sometimes welded up without this edge preparation, I prefer to bevel even this thin stuff.) Even with the bevel, a gap of about 1mm. should also be left between the plates to ensure complete penetration and to avoid distortion. And if the gap is lost, either by inaccurate cutting, or by heat distortion, then it must be ground out using a very thin cutting disc in the grinder. Unless this is done, the weld bead can just sit on top of the plates, and when ground off there may be very little holding the two bits of steel together. This can obviously lead to weeping at the seams and ultimate fracture.

Plating Sequence

If strip-chine construction is being used, the chine plate will be the first to go up. And this may almost be regarded as part of the framing process with the plate in the role of a bilge stringer.

But with the other methods of construction that we looked at in Chapter 5, there is no hard and fast rule as to the order of plating. There is a lot to be said in favour of putting the deck plates on first as this can stiffen up the whole framework before the more rigorous plating begins. An additional advantage to this approach is that laying the deck is much easier if the plates can overlap the edge and then be trimmed to size. This will not be possible if the topside plates with bulwarks or toe rail incorporated are already *in situ*.

It is usual to begin the hull plating in the middle of the ship so as to lock in the initial stresses there rather than at the ends. And it is necessary to match each plate fitted with its brother on the opposite side of the boat, again to prevent undue concentration of stress and to prevent frame distortion. Accordingly, when the plate on one side has been offered up and then cut, its opposite number can be cut out to match—provided you are confident both sides are exactly the same. If in doubt, make a template first, or offer up the plate separately to both sides. Remember, once a plate is incorrectly cut it becomes just scrap. It isn't possible satisfactorily to fill large gaps with weld metal for anything other than a very short run.

Only ease of construction dictates whether to fit the topside or bottom plates first, and the topsides would seem to be the best choice. With the bottom plates in first you would spend a lot of time climbing in and out, although against that, the bottom would provide a solid base on which to stand when clamping up the topsides.

Tools

For plating you need a few specialist tools in addition to those we have already looked at. More cost you say, but don't panic, because most of what you need can be made cheaply from offcuts. Plenty of the clamps that we made up in Chapter 3 now become necessary; twenty or more won't go amiss. But you will also need other bits and pieces to persuade the plate into its rightful place snug up to the framing. 'Dogs' are useful, and these can be cut out of scrap 5mm. plate as in Fig. 43. These dogs are tacked to the plate so that the right angle

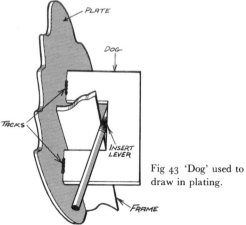

Fig 43 'Dog' used to draw in plating.

goes behind the frame, and then a lever can be inserted and the plate pulled back and tacked. The dog is then broken off the plate by knocking against its tack. It is useful to make up a selection of dogs with different length arms so that plate can be drawn in from any distance.

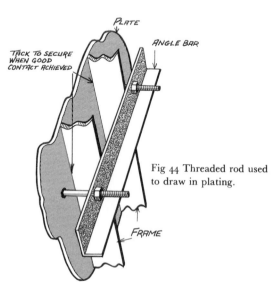

Fig 44 Threaded rod used to draw in plating.

A more sophisticated way of doing the same job is to use threaded steel rod. Two lengths are tacked to the plate either side of a pair of frames, and angle bar, with holes drilled appropriately, is fitted on to the rods. The angle is then progressively tightened up against the frame with nuts, drawing the plate home as in Fig. 44. The threaded rod approach allows very precise movement of the plate, which enables gradual bending to the hull shape. And the steel is always under control, whereas levers and props have a habit of slipping, sometimes with dangerous results. But using a prop and wedges to force the plate up against the frames from outside does mean you don't have to make tacks which can often pucker the plate and may be visible when the hull is painted.

Plate Bending
Although it may be impossible to flex some plates in heavily shaped areas with compound curvature (perhaps at the ends) by using cold-bending techniques, it should seldom be

38 Plating. Levers and props are useful, but they can slip.

necessary to have these pieces rolled, as there are several other possibilities. Perhaps the best method is to template as accurately as possible and fit the plate in the normal way, pulling it as close as possible with the threaded rods. When it won't go any nearer, then the oxy-acetylene torch comes out to heat the metal at critical areas. If extra pull is applied while the metal is hot, little by little the plate should bend into shape. Most curves can be achieved in this way, but it is a long process. An alternative is to slit the plate at points where it won't bend, and then weld together again after it is in position, but this is messy and shouldn't really be necessary. A final alternative for areas that are obviously going to be difficult is to use a succession of thin strips which will easily be bent one at a time. This means a lot of welding, but may be the only way for a really tricky curve. It should not be required if the hull has been designed with steel's limitations in mind, and it's worth checking this out before finally choosing a set of plans.

Fitting the Plates

Steel plates are heavy. Not only are they difficult to move about, but if they get out of control an edge can make a very passable guillotine. So the message is that they must not be allowed to get out of control at any time. That means careful handling, and it also means having the proper *lifting gear*.

To move plate from the cutting-out floor to the building site, rollers are useful. Sophisticated rollers in a frame are fine, but plenty of offcuts of steel tube of approximately 2in. diameter will probably serve just as well. Plate is always best moved by rolling rather than lifting: if it is lifted it can fall. But some sort of lifting tackle is necessary at the fitting stage and the simple eight/ten part tackles that are commonly sold for lifting out car engines should do fine for the job. Two or three would be useful, and you will need some point to hang them from, although if you are building indoors that should not present a problem. But remember to check that the beam you use has ample strength to cope with the 160 pounds of an 8ft. × 4ft. × ⅛in. plate. In the open you have more of a problem and a gantry is really necessary unless you can afford the luxury of a mini-mobile crane for the few days of the topside and deck plating work. The gantry will have to be movable and so constructed that there is no possibility of it falling over. These requirements make it into a fairly sophisticated piece of apparatus so an alternative is really needed. If you have not plated the deck already, it is possible to weld girder section vertically to the frames and deck beams and use this to achieve the hoist. The danger here is the risk of frame distortion. The best answer I suppose might be an army of strong men to lift the plates into position and a band of willing helpers ready with the clamps. But they are not always available. A useful trick when raising steel plates into position is to weld a length or two of angle just below the required position of the plate. The web of the angle should point upwards so as to form a trough into which the plate can fit without escaping. If the angle is sloped in towards the hull, the plate will fall into place with its own gravity. It can be tapped forward or aft precisely into the right spot, and then clamped up ready for tacking.

The bottom plates are not so much of a problem, as for one thing there isn't so far to lift them. I have a hydraulic trolley jack which I have found excellent for raising these plates slowly and safely, but bottle jacks aren't so good as they are prone to toppling over. A perfectly good alternative is to weld eyes to the inside of the plate, and use the tackle to lift the steel snug up against the frames. Possible puckering of the plate by welding on the eyes will not be visible as it will be below the waterline.

Tacking the Plates
Even a few tacks will stiffen up the hull enormously, so it is

essential to check that the frames are absolutely fair before striking up the welder. Any unfairness should become readily apparent as the plates are clamped up, if it hasn't already been spotted and rectified with the use of a fairing batten. Best to stand well back from a newly clamped up plate and eye it down its length to make absolutely sure it looks pretty.

Before tacking make sure the seam is perfectly level by applying a straight edge across the join. It is best to start your tacks in the middle of the seam and work progressively outwards, first to one side of the middle and then to the other. Spacing can be fairly wide at first (6 inches or so) and then filled in prior to final welding, so that the final spaces are about 3 inches. It may be necessary to use spacers to stop the gap closing as the tacks are made. Pieces of thin welding rod will serve for this purpose. The plate seams are best welded up before extensive tacking to the frames, but some local tacks will be needed to hold the plates in position while the clamps are removed. Keep these locating tacks to a minimum until the whole is strengthened by plating: this will help prevent distortion of the frames. No final welding should be considered until the entire hull is plated.

The Final Welding

Diligent work up to now, not to mention a lot of expensive material, can be ruined by carelessness at this final stage. Nor should you think that hiring a professional welder will necessarily ensure success. Many welders, as opposed to platers, are used to having to lay down as much weld metal as possible, in the shortest possible time. This is exactly what you don't want for a plating job. *Short runs*, the *minimum application of heat* and a *properly controlled welding sequence* are the keys to success. And this is because when metal is melted, it shrinks; as much as one inch in fifty if a complete rod is melted, though much less where the melted piece is constrained by solid metal attached (i.e. a weld); here the shrinkage can be around 0·1 per cent. But the restraint of the surrounding plate can set up stresses at the weld which, if excessive, can ultimately lead to fracture under load. The less the heat, the smaller the stresses, and a proper welding sequence will even out those that do occur. It is impossible to eradicate excessive shrinkage and the resulting stresses and distortion once they have occurred.

In order to keep the heat application down to a minimum, the amperage of the welder must be kept as low as possible, consistent with a satisfactory weld. This means using small rods, and I would not consider larger than 12s; size 14 is often entirely suitable. The technique of skip-welding is also necessary to minimize the heat applied to a given area. Runs of no more than 3 inches are used (2 inches might be better on thin plate), applied first to one then to the other side of the middle of the seam. Gaps of the same length as the run are left to be filled by the next sequence of runs. This procedure is tedious as each run must be chipped and brushed to remove the slag, and there will be a great many 3in. runs in a 40-foot boat. Nevertheless, if skip-welding is not strictly followed, the plates will inevitably buckle and that will be very noticeable after painting. I thought I knew better than my shipwright tutor on one deck job, and used up a complete rod before stopping. The resulting distortion annoys me to this day.

A useful technique to keep plates fair by way of a weld, is to tack pieces of flat bar vertically, at a right angle across the seam while work is in progress. This serves to minimize the shrinkage and resulting inward buckling that can so easily occur. Remember to tack on one side of the bar only, so that a bash with the hammer against the tacks will readily break them away.

Ideally, tacking should all have been done on the inside of the plate so that the outside skip-welding can be free from interruption by the tack blobs. This also achieves an equalizing of the welding on the inside and outside of the hull. It is the outside run that needs to be perfect to prevent weeping at the seams; the inside run is just a back-up. But tacking on the inside like this can sometimes be difficult, especially when short-handed. So provided outside tacks are properly de-slagged there should be no real problems, as the distance between two such tacks will be about the length of a skip-weld.

It is best to alternate from port to starboard. And while it is clearly too tedious to swop sides for every skip-weld sequence, no more than one plate should be welded up before moving across. A good idea if two machines and operators are available is to set one to work on each side.

When all the seams are completed, it is time to fair the plates, and this should be done before the frames are welded solid.

Fairing-in the Plates

Fairing-in can only be done satisfactorily before the framework is welded solid, and in frameless construction it is done after the frames have been removed; and therein lies one of the advantages of this approach. It is much easier to fair-in plates if they are not constrained by runs of flat bar, whether welded solid or not.

Some lack of fairness may be regarded as almost inevitable, no matter how much care is taken in the welding. And there are various corrective methods, although none can cope with excessive distortion. A common problem is weld shrinkage at seams, which causes the plates to bow inwards. This should be prevented on transverse butts by using the technique of flat bar stretched across, already described. And in Chapter 7 I discussed the idea of minimizing the need for such butts by using continuous lengths of plate. Distortion at longitudinal butts is not quite so eye-catching.

Where shrinkage has caused an inward bow it may be

removed by stretching the weld or shrinking the rest of the plate. But the shrinking method is really possible only in very local areas. The shrinking technique involves heating up the area of the inward bow by first circling an oxy-acetylene torch over it until the whole area becomes red hot, and then cooling it rapidly by quenching with water. This will cause some contraction which should reduce the bow, but the procedure may need to be repeated a number of times. The better alternative is weld stretching, and this is achieved by using a hefty hammer on the inside of the plate in conjunction with a dolly against the outside. The dolly is needed to prevent distortion at the point of impact. If this work is done slowly and systematically, it is possible to stretch the welds until they conform to the rest of the plating. Ear plugs are a good idea!

Once the fairing is completed, the plates can be welded finally to the frames, assuming the method of construction calls for the framework to be left in. Only battleships require

39 Skip-welding on a deck beam.

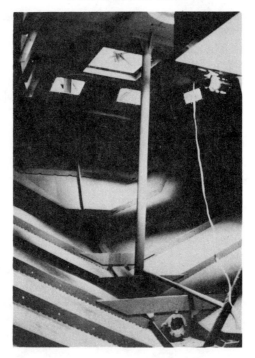

40 Frames 'stitch'-welded to the plate in order to
minimize heat distortion.

plates continuously welded to their frames. In small boats
with their thin plate, the excess application of heat needed for
such welds could result in a weaker, not a stronger job.
Accordingly skip-welds are again used. Starting from the
middle of the frame, short runs of about 2 inches should be
made first one side of the frame, and then the other. These
runs can be made opposite each other or staggered.

Every effort must be made to minimize the temperature
rise at any one spot. This means working to a strict sequence,
so that adjacent areas have a chance to cool down. It may be

useful to mark up the sequence on the plate before commencing work, but unless you keep a strict control on local heating, the all too common 'washboard' effect will be produced with the ribs more prominent than those on the hungriest of horses. There is some advantage in welding the longitudinals before the transverse frames. This is because distortion in a fore-and-aft direction is much less noticeable to the eye than vertical distortion. Also weld shrinkage on transverse frames can sometimes pull the frames out of vertical alignment.

Distortion at the frames is more difficult to eradicate. Heat shrinkage will sometimes work and fitting a local stringer may sometimes help to force a bow into the right shape, but this looks a bodge to anyone who knows. The real answer is not to let it occur and this means minimum welding at the frames with scrupulous attention to the welding sequence.

Filler

'If all else fails, there is always the filler', seems to be the policy of some yards. I hate the stuff and would not have it anywhere near a boat of mine. I would far rather see a slight wobble in my plating than contemplate the risk of filler fall-out and consequent corrosion such as described by Eric Hiscock in *Sou' West in 'Wanderer IV'*! Hiscock reports that his Dutch builder had applied the dreaded stuff contrary to a specific request, not only above the waterline but below as well. Above the waterline is bad enough, but below seems pointless, as ripples can hardly offend the eye down there. Dutch yards do produce lovely fair hulls, but to my cynical eye a too-perfect steel hull smacks of filler, and I am interested to know what the filler hides.

Decks

In Chapter 9, I suggested making up the deck beams as part of the frame hoop, but I will now have another look at the beams in the context of the decks that sit on them. Decks lack the shape strength of hulls, and accordingly need greater support or greater inherent strength in the decking material. Thus Lloyd's rules require heavier beams than frames, but that is not normally convenient to the small-craft builder who will prefer to use the same size. This should not normally be a problem provided the decks are beefed up by suitable inclusion of bulkheads or larger beams at masts or other stress points. But there will be a problem if the frames are widely spaced (anything more than 18 inches should be checked). In this case, either extra beams must be included between the frames, or you must use heftier beams plus stringers to cope with sag. I prefer this latter method as the stringers will readily fall to the fore-and-aft shape of the deck without prior bending. On the other hand these deeper beams might just take that extra bit of headroom you were looking for.

Flat bar beams are perfectly satisfactory if a steel deck is to be used, but angle will obviously be necessary with plywood or planks, in order to provide points of attachment. The angle will have to be bent so as to present a flat surface to the deck and this is its weakest direction. Accordingly, if angle is used for the frames with the web inboard, then the beams ought really to be made out of heftier section to avoid a weak point.

Sometimes wooden deck beams are used with wooden

decks but I fail to see the point. These beams will take longer to laminate and while they can themselves have sufficient strength, the join to the frame can be weak. And this is exactly where strength is required. It is marginally easier to screw the deck down than to bolt through, but that is a trivial gain. A more significant advantage is that it may not be necessary to line the deckhead, especially if the beams are made up out of attractive hardwoods. Simply varnish the beams and paint between; or paint the lot.

Deck Materials

The choice is between steel, plywood or wood planks, or steel with wood laid on top. There will be very little difference in cost between ply and steel, and fitting time should be roughly the same, although someone not familiar with steelwork who buys a hull for fitting out might find a time advantage in favour of ply. But normally the deciding factors will be strength and weight. Steel has a considerable advantage in terms of strength as it makes the whole hull into one integral unit each part giving support to the other. Plywood, if well bolted and used in large sheets, can have something of the same effect but planks add virtually no stiffness, so you will be relying almost entirely on the beams. Accordingly if laid decks are required, it is not satisfactory to fit straight on to the beams, so a different method is required and this is discussed later (p. 172).

The weight of a steel deck can sometimes make the boat crank. Four mm. steel is roughly equivalent in weight to 30mm. plywood, but while 4mm. steel would be reasonable for most small craft, 20mm. plywood would be ample for yachts up to 40 feet and this would comply with Lloyd's. It should not sag even with comparatively wide beam spacing (60cm.). Plywood being thicker, is stiffer and accordingly ply can afford a valuable 33 per cent weight saving; and on smaller boats, it could be used at a thickness as little as

16mm., thereby increasing the saving. Three mm. steel would theoretically give an obvious 25 per cent reduction in weight on 4mm., but will tend to sag between beams so that it will be difficult to achieve a fair deck. Accordingly, narrow beam spacing or stringers are necessary, and either can nullify the weight reduction.

I prefer steel for decks, not only because of its strength, but also because of the ease of adding deck-houses and fittings and the certainty of complete watertightness. Deck-houses and fittings can be welded straight to a steel deck, but would have to be bolted to ply, producing a weak point and a leak point. The only time I would consider ply is on a flush-deck boat, and even then precautions should be taken. The ply must clearly be of marine grade (B.S. 1088 in England) and should be bought sufficiently wide to span the deck as it is essential for strength to avoid longitudinal butts. The manufacturers produce their ply in 8ft. × 4ft. sheets, but these can be scarfed together at the factory at comparatively little extra cost, although usually with some time delay. One and a half sheets should just span the average deck, but remember that at least 6 inches could be lost in the scarfing.

Joining transverse butts can be a problem (when will they invent rods that weld wood!). They cannot be joined over a deck beam as that will not provide room for the double line of fastenings. One good idea is to fit steel stringers across the join, but this can lose some of the weight advantage. An alternative is to put plywood straps under the deck, but these will need to be quite wide; perhaps as wide as the beam spacing. As these should cover the complete join and be almost as thick as the deck itself, steel stringers would probably turn out lighter. They would almost certainly be easier to fit.

Choice of fastening for the ply is another problem. Screws up from below are possible, but only with stout plywoods of say 20mm. (¾in.). Bolts are stronger, but they can cause

170

leaks, they are more difficult to fit and they cost more. The leak problem can be solved by countersinking and filling (necessary anyway); the fitting should not prove too difficult if two people are available, but the cost of the bolts could be enormous. Mild steel bolts are cheaper, but I hesitate to recommend them because of the danger of corrosion. The cost of stainless bolts could well point you back towards a steel deck. And even with stainless, electrolysis can prove a problem, although collars can be obtained to insulate the bolts.

Ply tends to leak at the edges and if the edges are allowed to get wet and stay wet delamination could follow. It is best not to butt ply with vertical edges, as the joint can never be so perfect as to prevent a thin gap in which water could collect. Better to bevel the edges as for welding, and fill the bevel with a flexible seam-filling compound such as Jeffrey's Seamflex. This will cope with slight flexing of the ply and will not deteriorate. Exposed ply at deck edges can be coped with in the same way as at joins. Fig. 45 illustrates a method of obtaining a watertight joint between plywood decks and steel sides. The topside plate can, if required, be extended up above the deck to form a bulwark with the edge capped.

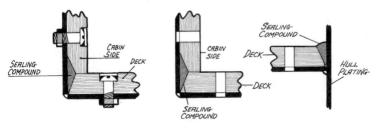

Fig 45 Watertight deck joints.

Deck Sheathing

Plywood and even steel decks can usefully be sheathed in fibreglass, the former to prevent leaks and the latter to prevent corrosion. Although the initial cost for materials will be quite high, taken against long-term maintenance the investment is probably worthwhile. One problem can be how to finish off the edges of the fibreglass, but such things as toe rails or rubbing strakes can be utilized to hide and protect these vulnerable areas.

Composite sheathing compounds can be obtained, and most of these are attractive, very hard wearing, and protect steel decks from corrosion. They go on thick, so they give some sound and temperature insulation. But they are expensive. Not as expensive as a wooden laid deck, although getting on that way. Such deck coverings as Trakmark are a cheaper alternative and give some of the same advantages. These are stuck on, so they are hard wearing and do protect the decks against the inevitable chips and scrapes, providing at the same time an excellent non-slip surface. However, they are prone to lifting from the deck, so scrupulous attention to the glueing job is required. For me, I'd choose a good quality epoxy deck paint, but more about that in Chapter 15.

Teak Laid Decks

Teak laid decks look beautiful. They are also incredibly expensive, (Iroko is a cheaper and satisfactory alternative), require frequent attention and can add considerably to the deck weight. So I would have nothing to do with them. But for those who can't resist that luxury look, there are a few considerations to be taken into account. The woodwork side I don't pretend to be able to cover (try Chapelle's *Boat Building*), but securing the wood to the deck affects the steelwork. If teak is being laid over the top of steel it is obviously purely decorative and not intended to give any structural support. It can accordingly be kept thin. A quarter of an inch is about the minimum thickness though, and even this can present fixing and splitting problems. This thin stuff can be simply stuck to the deck using one of the modern epoxy glues, and, provided the job is done thoroughly, corrosion should not form underneath. But I wouldn't have much confidence in the lifespan of such a job, and I have met several owners who have come unstuck with this sort of deck!

If thicker wood is used it can be snugged down on bedding compound with countersunk bolts, but the hundreds of holes that will be required in the deck are bound to cause leaks sooner or later. A better but more sophisticated alternative is a machine which spot-welds studs through the wood on to the deck. Only one or two yards of my acquaintance have these machines but it seems the best answer if you can afford it. Sometimes plywood is laid on the steel first, and the teak laid on top. This means that very thin teak can be glued and screwed on to the ply quite quickly, but half-inch ply is about the minimum to provide any grip for the screws. This, plus quarter-inch teak, and the steel, adds up to a very heavy deck indeed. Eric Hiscock attributed the initial crankiness of *Wanderer IV* to this cause. No, if you want teak, then the answer is to have a ply deck and not a steel one. If you do that, the ply can be reduced to about 12mm. ($\frac{1}{2}$in.), provided that the teak is also at least that thickness.

Deck-edges

In Chapter 9 I looked at how sheer stringers could be made to finish off deck-edges. Fig. 46 shows some more examples.

The oval tube could look quite nice, but I don't much care for the angle bar alternatives. Angle is difficult to bend in a fair curve and has sharp corners. I much prefer tube in one form or another as this is easy to bend to a nice fair curve and has no corners. Box section doesn't seem easy to bend, and the one example I saw had its sheer broken in about six places.

If you don't want a sheer stringer the following are the usual alternatives.

Fig. 46 (j) has a lot to commend it in terms of construction. If the decks are plated first, then the hull plating can be extended above the required sheerline which can then be faired in by eye and cut exactly to shape with the grinder. The plate edge can be finished off with round bar, oval tube or even box section. Oval is the traditional finish, and perhaps looks the best.

Fig. 46 (k) is a much stronger weld, and the alternative (l) could lead to a weakness, especially if the outside weld is ground down, prior to painting the hull. Additionally, the

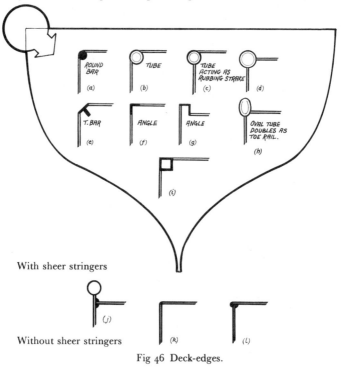

With sheer stringers

Without sheer stringers

Fig 46 Deck-edges.

recommended joint gives a more rounded edge which will keep paint on better.

Toe rails can be added where the plating doesn't create them. Flat bar with the edges rounded to keep the paint on serves well for this job. But a nice alternative is one I saw on *Joshua* and that is flat bar with holes pre-drilled all the way along. It looked good and made perfect anchoring points for sheet leads and the like (photo 41).

41   Toe rail made of flat bar with holes pre-drilled.

Rubbing Strakes

I don't like them. A nicely varnished teak rubbing strake looks fabulous—so long as its owner keeps it firmly tied up in the marina. But as soon as it makes contact with its first lock or quay wall then it starts to look tatty; worse, it sticks out and can easily catch on things. That's what fenders are for, you say, so why do you need a rubbing strake? One reason, I suppose, might be that fitting a strake can break up excessive areas of topside. But a tastefully painted sheerline could serve just as well.

Another problem with wooden rubbing strakes is how to fix them. Bolts through the side is the usual method, but this can lead to leaks, and all the ceiling will have to be taken down if the strake is damaged. Studs welded on are better, but difficult to replace if damaged. Best is to bolt downwards through two pieces of flat bar welded to the side of the hull.

Metal strakes are a better idea altogether and in Chapter 9 we saw how the sheer stringer could be made to double for this purpose. If strakes are used, they are best painted a contrasting dark colour, not only for appearance's sake, but also to hide the inevitable scratches.

Rubbing strakes are sometimes welded to the outside of the hull plating, and *Abraxis* had acquired these before we acquired her. Half round bar is normally used, and this can be made to act as an external longitudinal stringer. However, the bar has to be welded all round and this can cause plate shrinkage and distortion.

12

Deck Fittings

All sorts of boaty bits can be fabricated very cheaply out of odd scraps of steel. And in the process a considerable amount of money can be saved. It is best to have your creations galvanized as it is very difficult to keep paint on them. The main thing to remember before galvanizing is that the steel must be scrupulously clean of paint. Rust is all right as it is removed by the acid bath, but the acid won't touch paint. It is often useful to have an eye on the top of a bollard to attach a block for such things as extra sheet leads or boom guys. This should be done before the job is sent for galvanizing. A useful way of obtaining eyes is to cut ⅜in. chain links in half—chandleries that sell chain are often able to make you a present of these half links.

Bollards
Bollards of many shapes and sizes can be made out of offcuts of galvanized gas barrel or scaffold poles. The pipe is first cut to a suitable length (best to be too short rather than too tall from a looks point of view) and can then either be welded to the deck or to a base-plate if the deck is not steel. Many designs can be invented but Fig. 47 shows a few I have seen. My favourites are (1) and (2), with (2) making a really secure moor. To make the curved top (for elegance, to keep paint on and to prevent excessive chafe) cut a piece of thick steel to the internal diameter of your tube and weld all round with several runs if necessary, so as to give a slope. It is then a simple matter to run the grinder round the top to fair it off.

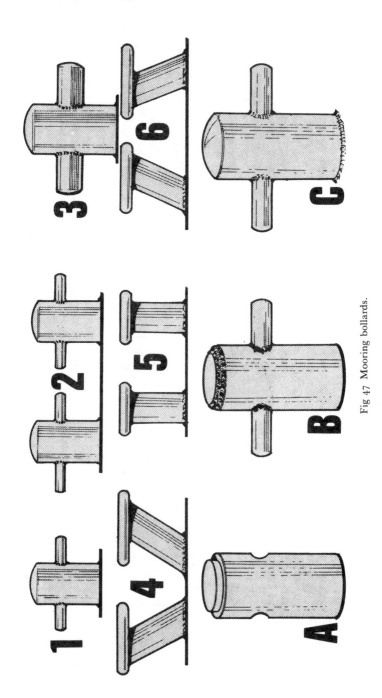

Fig 47 Mooring bollards.

For the centre bar, 12mm. diameter is reasonable. It is best to drill a couple of holes in the tube so that the bar can be pushed all the way through and then welded at either side. It is impossible to weld bar to each side but it can be difficult to get a really strong weld and to keep the bar straight.

Bollard (3) shows a grown-up version of (1) and (2). It can be used as a towing bollard or as a strong point on the foredeck. A large size gas barrel is used here with the top domed as before. Smaller-sized barrel can then be cut to length and welded on either side with its ends domed as well. Bollards (4), (5) and (6) are supposedly more modern in appearance and they are arguably better for surging rope. Thick plate is welded this time over the top of the barrel, and the edges are ground off. With (4) and (6) the plate is fitted so as to give a wider lip on the side where the rope will ride up the slope of the barrel. Bollard (5) isn't much use to my mind as you can't really attach a line to it if it comes at an angle down to the deck. Many mooring situations are like this and of course the rope could just pull off under tension.

Photo 42 of the foredeck arrangement on the *Joshua*-class *Vega*, illustrates an interesting bollard and chain snubber.

42 Foredeck on *Joshua*-class *Vega*, showing bollard
and chain snubber.

Cleats

Cleats are very easy to make by taking a piece of about 12mm. round bar and bending to a suitable shape. If you want several, it is best to make up a jig around which to bend them. The jig can consist of round bar welded at appropriate intervals to a piece of heavy scrap plate. Heat is necessary to bend the bar without introducing stress cracks, so oxy-acetylene gear would be useful. If it is not available, it may well be worthwhile to obtain a carbon arc torch for use with the arc welder. This device produces a flame from the arc which is well suited to heating and brazing tasks, although it is not suitable for welding. To finish the cleats, it is as well to taper them and round off the ends, using the grinder. The tapering is largely aesthetic, but the rounded ends help to prevent chafe. The cleats can be welded straight to the deck or if the decks aren't steel, it will be necessary to weld on a base-plate through which bolt holes can be drilled.

In some cases it may be necessary to strengthen the deck under bollards or cleats. Our big mooring bollard on the foredeck is strengthened by a pair of stringers running underneath and joined to the deck-beams. But our cleats for springs are not strengthened as they are close to the deck-edges which provide angular reinforcement, and the decks are of comparatively thick $\frac{3}{16}$in. steel. With thinner plate it may be advisable to use stringers.

Chain Plates

On many steel boats you will see chain plates which are just pieces of flat bar welded to the side of the boat so that a couple of inches protrude at the top, through which a hole is drilled to take the bottlescrew. This is undoubtedly simple and it does work. The main thing to watch when fitting is that the angle of the plate is parallel to the direction of the load. Lower shroud plates, for example, will therefore be at a slight angle to the vertical.

But I mistrust this system, because of an experience we had while beating south along the Frisian Islands. Unknown to me the foremast upper shroud chain plate parted at the point where it met the deck. I didn't discover it until we had reached harbour, when I promptly turned green, as the genoa and fisherman had obviously been hanging on a mast supported only by the lowers for an unknown period of time (praise be to telegraph poles!). The problem had been crevice corrosion at the point where the chain plate joined the deck. An athwartship strain had probably enhanced the deterioration. For the trip back from Den Helder I put lashings on all the other shrouds in case any more of them went. On reaching England I chipped off the paint around the chain plates and found that all of them had suffered some rusting, but that they could be strengthened by building up the joint between chain plate and deck with a fillet-weld. I was content with this for the lowers, but decided that only a renewal of the upper shroud chain plates would give me real confidence. Instead of plates I opted for galvanized flanges welded to the deck-edge in a way that would obviate corrosion. (See photo 43 of broken chain plate and the eye-flange that replaced it.)

43 *Abraxis.* Eye-flange replacing broken chain plate.

Guardrails

Stanchions are often used as an attachment point for the upper shrouds on Dutch-built steel boats. The reason for this is so that the attachment point for the shroud can be at exactly the same height as the tabernacle pivot bolt for the mast. This allows the mast to be lowered while keeping tension on the shrouds, thereby maintaining control. If stanchions are to double as shroud attachment points in this way they must be strengthened by triangulation (photo 44). Additionally, I would prefer to see a triangular gusset-plate going inboard as in photo 45.

44 Stanchion acting as shroud attachment point.

Many people don't like to see ordinary stanchions welded straight to the deck, arguing that the attachment point is subject to corrosion and that the whole tube may need replac-

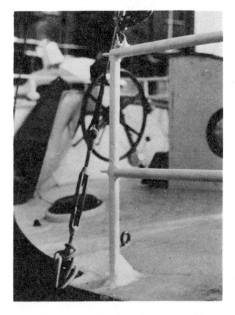

45 Stanchion with triangular gusset-plate.

ing after even minor damage. It is true that corrosion can be a problem at the base, and as much from the inside as from the outside. Although the outside can be protected by scrupulous maintenance of the paint coating, the inside needs protection at the building stage. So galvanized tube should be used and it is better if partly filled with paint or pitch after it has been welded to the deck, to protect the inside from any moisture which gets in.

Those who don't like the idea of fixed stanchions may prefer to weld tube sockets to the deck so that the stanchion will just fit inside, where it may be locked with a split pin through both tubes (photo 46). Spare stanchions can then be carried on board and replacement is a matter of minutes. The same result is achieved by welding a spigot of round bar to

183

the deck, and slipping the stanchion over it. The latter looks neater, and the only disadvantage with either method is the fact that it is difficult to prevent rust from appearing around the base. A spigot cannot be strengthened with a gusset, which may be a problem with tall stanchions.

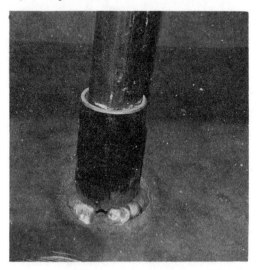

46 Guardrail stanchion inside welded tube socket.

The guardrails on *Abraxis* are of welded tube all the way round the ship, with gateways on each side and at the stern. They give an immense feeling of confidence, are useful for points of attachment and I would have no other system. There are problems, though, such as susceptibility to damage while alongside and the difficulty of keeping paint on. It is especially difficult to get paint to stick on newly galvanized rails, so they are best let weather for a while to allow the acids to be released before painting. (Alternatively etching primers are available to achieve the same end, although I have not always found them to be successful.)

These solid rails don't really suit small boats and can give large ones a rather rugged appearance. They contribute a lot to our 'battleship' image. The alternative is wire, which tends to be a lot less obtrusive. The wire can be attached to each stanchion in a number of ways, the simplest of which is by holes drilled through. This has the disadvantage that the wire must be unthreaded if a stanchion needs replacing, and it is also very difficult to keep paint on around the holes which are in any event a point of access for moisture. An alternative is channelling welded to the top of the stanchion into which the wire is laid and lashed. The middle guardrail can be threaded through eyes welded to the inside of the stanchion, the eyes being cut off should the stanchion need replacing. The top rail could be secured in the same way.

If a solid rail is not wanted I would choose flexible stainless wire. Galvanized wire just doesn't last in this job and the plastic-covered sort is positively unsafe. The trouble with the plastic-covered wire is partly that you can't see what is happening to it underneath its covering, but more specifically the joint with the usual Norseman type terminal is highly vulnerable. Usually a slight gap is left between the plastic covering and the terminal, and it is there that corrosion can get a rapid grip. This was brought home to me on a Yachtmaster practical course that I attended, where the skipper-owned tuition boat was fitted with this wire. Several of us pointed out that the wires were badly rusted at the terminals, but the skipper was convinced that they were all right as they had been fitted less than a year before. But one of them did break during the week, and a crew member was very lucky not to end up in the water. And a brand new Maxi 9·5 that we waved off on a long voyage had the tell-tale rust marks at the terminals. At the risk of labouring the point, I repeat my opinion that this type of wire has no place on a serious cruising boat.

Pulpits

Pulpits are not difficult to make out of tubular steel: the only real problem is to get them to look nice. I prefer to make them out of slightly larger o.d. pipe than the stanchions as they are more vulnerable and greater reliance is placed on them. Don't make the mistake of selecting too thin-walled pipe on the basis that it will be easier to bend, as this will lead to problems in welding and an inherent weakness. A pipe-bender is very useful for the job, if not essential. They can be hired for a small sum and other odds and ends could be bent up at the same time. Doing the job by hand often leads to kinks which make the product look a bodge.

Bowsprits and Bowsprit Fittings

Many cruising boat designs have provision for a bowsprit which spreads the base of the sail plan and enables the use of shorter masts. Bowsprits are easy to make up out of steel, using the multi-purpose steel tube. The simplest method is a large-diameter tube welded to the bow, with a bobstay of wire, chain, tube or round bar coping with the upward pull of

47 *Joshua*-class boat with A-frame bowsprit.
(Note all the ancillary fittings.)

48 *Abraxis*. The bowsprit has steel flats welded along the top
of the tubes to enable teak slats to be fitted.

the forestay. Unless the tube is very short you will also need
shrouds back to either side of the hull to prevent sideways
movement. This single tube system can be vulnerable.
Bernard Moitessier's *Joshua* had this type of bowsprit and it
was badly damaged by a freighter during the single-handed
round-the-world race, whereas an A-frame bowsprit would
arguably have stood a better chance of escaping unharmed.
In fact subsequent boats built to the *Joshua* design have had
the A-frame bowsprit (see photograph 47). This takes the
form of two tubes welded down either side of the bow and
connected at the outboard end by a short piece of tubing. On
Abraxis flat bar is welded to the tubes so that teak slats can be
bolted on. This makes a good working platform when surrounded by a protective pulpit, although the platform can
sometimes slam in a head sea.

187

A more elegant appearance can be obtained by creating a clipper bow out of steel and finishing it off with beautifully carved trail boards. The Hiscocks' *Wanderer IV* has this fine arrangement, incorporating a neat anchor stowage. However, Eric does make the comment that the square section, on which *Wanderer*'s clipper bow is based, can tend to slam in heavy seas thereby impeding forward progress. He recommends that round section should be used.

The pretty Dutch steel yacht *Avalon* has a neat bowsprit arrangement designed by the owner and myself. The bowsprit (an addition to the original design) was to be of wood so that it could be steeved up in harbour. The bulwarks at the bows together with bow roller and chain plate had to be removed to make space for the bowsprit, and a channel-section housing for the spar was then fitted in their place. (Incidentally, for the cutting I used a hired BOC 'Portapak', as discussed in Chapter 3, and the oxygen bottle lasted just long enough to complete the work.) The roller was fitted by first welding up a channel-section with chain-retaining device as in Fig. 48. A hole was then drilled through both

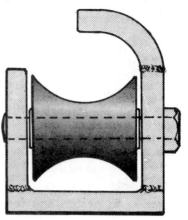

Fig 48 Bow roller.

sides of the channel so that a bolt could be pushed through with the roller threaded on. (A stainless bolt might have been best but we used galvanized.) The protruding bolt was ground flush and welded, prior to welding the complete job to the side of the channel bowsprit housing.

I spotted an unusual steel bowsprit on the American sloop *Cariad*. The single tubular design seemed quite normal from a distance, but closer inspection revealed that it was in fact telescopic! A second tube inside the first could be extended by a pulley system and then rigged in position to provide an immense bowsprit for setting extra sails in light weather. I understand that it didn't work that well in practice, but it is a very interesting idea!

Hawse Pipes

On a steel boat, anchor chains are commonly led aboard via a hawse pipe in the side of the hull. The pipe can either be right over the stem as in the photo 49, or to one side. Or

49 Hawse pipe right in the bows.

perhaps there could be one on either side in larger boats. The anchor can damage the paintwork while it is being hauled in, as it is difficult to control. But the stainless plate idea illustrated in the photograph is a good one, and can help to protect the hull. However, this type of installation necessitates the expense of a winch, as it isn't possible to get away with the chain snubber idea illustrated in photo 42 of the foredeck arrangement on *Vega*.

I prefer the simple bow roller format with an anchor stowed either side of the bowsprit as in *Wanderer IV*. But the chain still has to be fed down below. Care needs to be taken that the tube used is large enough for the job, and that there are no sharp bends before it reaches the chain locker. Our original hawse pipe was not much wider than the chain and it went vertically downwards with almost a right angle at the bottom to feed it into the locker. Crazy! Of course it jammed. This was especially a problem as our windlass was on top of the hawse pipe, so that if the chain jammed in the pipe, then the windlass wouldn't work. Accordingly you had to haul in by hand. A large-diameter pipe (at least three times the width of the chain) inclined at a slight angle directly into the locker solved the problem. And it is a problem that many people have experienced. Eric Hiscock had the same difficulty on *Wanderer IV*, and she was built in one of the foremost steel building yards. His solution was to cut out the pipe and build in a wooden chute instead.

Before we leave the subject of anchors, it is a good idea to protect the strip of foredeck where the chain normally bashes. We have no such protection, and the paint has a hard time. One way is to weld a thin stainless steel strip down the deck, and this can look quite smart. Alternatively, the deck coverings that were mentioned in the previous chapter (p. 172) will do the job.

Hatches, Doors and Companionways

Keeping hatches watertight can be a problem in any boat, and while no more difficult with steel, it may be considered more important as these are just about the only places where a steel boat can leak. Proprietary hatches are extremely expensive, so fabrication in steel would seem a reasonable choice. The main drawbacks are weight, and the difficulty of achieving a pleasing appearance.

When we bought *Abraxis*, all hatch-covers were steel and very heavy indeed. Each consisted of a welded frame with Perspex bolted to the inside and covered on the outside with a steel mesh. Rubber strip in channelling around the edge of the hatches seated down on to flat bar welded at right angles around the holes in the deck and formed the seal. The system was leak-proof and burglar-proof, but did make her look a bit like a prison ship. Worse, it could be positively dangerous as the means of securing open was inadequate. An engineer working on the boat in Burnham badly damaged his fingers when the hatch-cover came crashing down as he was climbing up the companionway. So the main hatch had to go. But the question of what to substitute for it occupied many a winter's evening. We eventually settled on a companion-type hatch (see photo 50), which we hoped would have a number

50 *Abraxis*. Companion-type main hatch.

of advantages. We reasoned that the washboards could be left out in most weathers, letting light and air into the cabin, and letting shouted instructions out of it, without the watch below getting soaked. We further argued that it would be fairly easy to open and close from the inside, unlike the previous hinged type which required superhuman strength to heave up from below. And above all it would be safe.

Two quotes I received for making up the companion were incredibly high. So I decided to have the pieces cut, and make the hatch myself. Each side was cut out as a quarter of a circle with a porthole in the middle. As we decided on $\frac{1}{8}$in. plate, the back and sliding parts had to be rolled so that they followed the same radius as the side plates. In fact the $\frac{1}{8}$in. plate was probably a mistake, as it has made the sliding part extremely heavy and not that easy to close. One-sixteenth-inch plate would have been amply strong and would have halved the weight. As we had the whole lot galvanized before it was welded to the deck, there would have been no real problem of corrosion on the thinner plate. Using the thinner stuff would, as an added benefit, have enabled us to bend the back and sliding plates by progressively welding around the radius, and so would have eliminated the need for rolling.

We originally planned to have doors to the scuttle but after many designs had been put on paper, we eventually settled for the simplicity of washboards. For slides to take the boards I welded channelling down the front edge on either side. To take the sliding hatch, I welded 1in. × $\frac{1}{8}$in. flat bar around the radius of the side plates on the outside. The hatch was located to these by angle bar rolled to the correct radius.

Had we not been able to get the angle bar rolled, I would have cut the appropriate radius out of $\frac{3}{16}$in. plate and then welded 1in. × $\frac{1}{8}$in. flat bar to it so as to form a right angle. The welding would have tended to distort the plate, so I would have tacked it at intervals to heavy scrap plate while the job was done. The welding would have had to be back-stepped with very short steps, allowing plenty of time for the metal to cool.

A metal-to-metal bearing surface for the hatch slides was clearly undesirable, so I obtained Tufnol strip from Thomas Foulkes in London, where the boat was lying at that time. This was very cheap and proved ideal for the job when through-bolted to the sideplates.

We decided to modify the forehatch rather than replace it, as it was much smaller and not often used, other than for letting air in. The mesh was the worst part of it, as it was impossible to keep painted especially on the underside. Accordingly, it looked a rusty mess most of the time, and considerably restricted the light. I took the angle-grinder to the mesh, and the hatch looked much better for it. But some sort of protection for the Perspex was still required, so I settled on galvanized round bar welded across with 4in. gaps. This has proved very satisfactory as the bars are amply strong, allow more light in, and don't shed rusty streaks all over the paintwork.

The rubber sealing strip in the channelling was in a terrible state and had to be replaced. I bought sufficient to do all the hatches a couple of times as sealing strip does not last very long. I have a habit of always doubling up when I buy parts, on the basis that if they have gone once they can go again.

The hinges for the hatch were badly corroded and had to be replaced. They have to be raised hinges so that the hatch clears the coaming as it is lifted. The hinges were easily made in the following fashion. I obtained $\frac{3}{8}$in. round bar and threaded 2 inches of tube on to it together with a nut at either end. I then bent the round bar as in Fig. 49, and welded the nuts solid then filed them round. This formed the basis of the hinge and when welded to the deck all that remained was to weld 2in. × 3in. × $\frac{3}{16}$in. flat bar to the tube and then to the hatch. I then drilled a small hole in the tube to allow a few

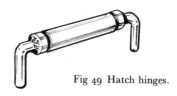

Fig 49 Hatch hinges.

spots of oil to be squirted in every now and again. The only problem with this arrangement is the possibility of rusting. The oil helps to prevent this and in any event it would take a considerable time for the hinge to deteriorate significantly. The job is so simple that replacement every five or ten years is no hardship. Stainless would have been better, but I did not have any. (Welding stainless to mild steel is not difficult with the right rods.)

Our *watertight doors* are made in a similar way to the forehatch. The hinges are exactly the same (I made up a lot of these in one go), as is the method of sealing. Two handles clamp the rubber sealing strip firmly to the angle bar coaming. The handles are simplicity itself, consisting of bent pieces of $\frac{1}{4}$in. × 1 in. flat bar bolted through the door as in Fig. 50. The clamping action is achieved by the handle closing on a wedge-shaped piece of steel.

Our *companion ladders* are all made out of steel naturally,

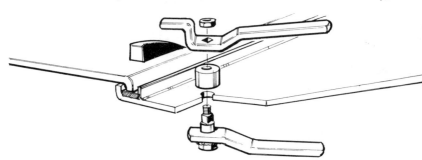

Fig 50 Hatch clamps.

and are very easy to produce. Box section seems to look better for this job than round tubing, so I would recommend using two bits of this cut to the appropriate length. Round bar of the appropriate width can then be welded between the two at top and bottom to provide a strong structure. Nine-inch intervals would be appropriate for the steps. So angle bar can be welded to both sides and 3in. × 1in. teak steps can then be bolted to the angle bar to make a strong attractive companionway. To secure, weld round bar to the sole (or concrete it in, if the sole is made of concrete) so that the box section just fits over. And the top, a hook and eye arrangement, can be welded on, as in Fig. 51. If the companion ladder is more than three or four rungs high, it may be as well to beef it up a bit by having two lengths of box section per side, secured together by the angle bar step supports.

Fig 51 Companion ladder.

Observation Domes

Observation domes (see photo 51) and hatches are becoming very popular now among ocean voyagers. One of the first to use them was the famous circumnavigator Bernard Moitessier in his ketch *Joshua*. He fitted one (made up out of a washing-up bowl!) for the trip Tahiti–Alicante by way of the Horn—see *Cape Horn: The Logical Route*. META (*Joshua*'s builders) now fit a more sophisticated version to all their voyaging boats. I made a similar version for *Abraxis* (photo 52), using an angle bar framework with Perspex bolted around the side. A conventional Simpson Lawrence aluminium hatch bolted to the top made the creation into an escape hatch and ventilator as well. We use this observation box for inside steering, and for standing watch in rough weather while under self-steering. And it works very well.

Several makes of dome are available, but they are not cheap.

Tabernacles and Mast Fittings

I have seen tabernacles of two basic types—plate or tube. They are very simple to make out of $\frac{1}{4}$in. plate, but perhaps

51 An 'Embrun' deck, from META. Note the hole in the foreground ready to accept an observation dome.

196

52 Observation dome for *Abraxis*.

look more elegant when made out of tube. Our main mast
tabernacle is made from 9in. diameter tube cut so as to allow
the heel of the mast to enter. Plate is welded to the inside so as
to prevent water collecting. Most mast fittings can be readily
fabricated out of steel. Starting from the top, our main
masthead fitting was made from steel tube, and fits over the
top of the wooden mast. The top is plated over to stop water
entering, and lugs are welded on all sides to take the shrouds
and stays. If masthead sheaves are to be incorporated, the
job becomes more complicated. Having done it on ours, I
believe that the traditional way of fitting them through the
mast itself is easier. I found it necessary to do the job in three
parts. First I welded a top on a 4in. length of pipe of the
appropriate diameter to fit over the mast, and drilled holes
all around the pipe for locating-screws. Next I cut off a length
of pipe, just longer than the diameter of the sheaves, and then
cut that vertically into four sections as in Fig. 52. The
centre-pieces were then ground down, taking off a little more
than the thickness of the sheaves. Four pieces of ⅜in. plate

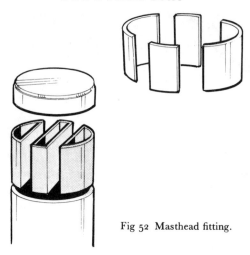

Fig 52 Masthead fitting.

were then cut to make the divisions between the sheaves which also serve to prevent the halyard wire jumping off. The four pieces of curved steel and the plate were then welded into three sections as in Fig. 52. These pieces were then welded to the original bit of pipe and a top plate was fitted. A further piece of pipe on top to take the lugs, with another plate on top, completed the body of the fitting. It only remained to fit the sheaves (galvanized not bronze for obvious reasons) by through-bolting with a stainless bolt.

The foremast fitting consists of a simple steel band set into the wood and secured by (but not supported by) screws. Lugs were welded on to take the shrouds/stays, and the sheaves were set into the wood.

Cross-tree supports can be many and varied. The simplest is probably the best, and I rather like the version on our foremast. Flat bar ($\frac{1}{4}$in. thick) is used to form the basis of the cross-tree attachment and to form the tang for the lower shrouds. The bar is through-bolted vertically to the mast and the bottom on each side is bent outwards and drilled to form a lug. A spigot of round bar is welded to it, and the spreader, which consists of thick-walled aluminium tube, simply fits over the end. Galvanized pipe could be used but would add unnecessarily to weight aloft. The danger of electrolysis between the round bar and the aluminium tube must be guarded against by taping the bar before fitting. This has the additional advantage of ensuring a snug fit.

Wooden spreaders can be secured in a number of ways of which the following are but two. The through-bolted flat bar idea could again be used, but this time with short lengths of box section welded to it. The wooden spreader will be cut square at the inboard end so that it fits into the box-section sockets where it can be secured by a pin. Alternatively, flat bar can be used to make straps at right angles to the mast and extending out along the cross-trees. They can be secured to the cross-trees by screws or through-bolting, and to the mast by notching in and screws. We have this system on the main mast and I am not that fond of it, although it does have the merit of being very simple. The problem is that the straps tend to pull away from the wood, but I hope that I shall overcome this by replacing the existing screws with bolts.

Davits

I am a bit prejudiced against davits on anything except quite large boats and they were one of the first things that I heaved overboard from *Abraxis*. But I might not have been so hasty had they not been a rather crude version consisting just of bent pipe. And I do think that davits on the stern are a good idea, and can achieve a useful increase in working space as well as making dinghy launching simple. However, they have the severe disadvantage of making the use of self-steering vane gear difficult, which put them out of the question for us. And I don't think that they are really suitable for ocean voyaging because of the danger from following seas.

Quite smart permanent davits can be fabricated fairly

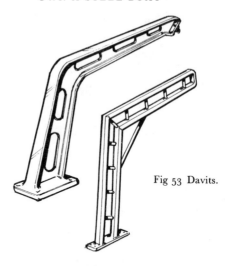

Fig 53 Davits.

quickly provided they are kept simple. The version in Fig. 53 can be constructed by cutting $\frac{1}{4}$in. plate to shape, and strengthening with $\frac{3}{16}$in. flat bar welded at right angles around the edge. Lightening holes, as in the diagram, improve the appearance (in my view) as well as saving weight. A simple method of construction, though perhaps not so pleasing in appearance, is to use a minimum ·61 in. box section doubled as is also shown in Fig. 53. The round bar triangulation in the diagram is an extra strength feature. It may not be necessary, depending on the weight of the dinghy, although it must be remembered that a heavy following sea can put a considerable strain on both the davits and the point of attachment. I would prefer to see davits bolted to the deck rather than welded straight on, as they are susceptible to damage and will sooner or later need to be removed for repair or replacement.

I have included just a selection of the bits and pieces that I have made. Numerous ideas will occur once you start to *think steel*. I reckon it is fair to say that virtually any boaty bit can be made, with a welder, a grinder and a few bits of steel.

13

Fitting Out

I don't intend to cram the sum total of human knowledge on fitting out into this one chapter. There are plenty of good books on this subject alone (I mention one or two in the Bibliography). So most of my remarks are directed towards the problems and advantages that are specific to fitting out a steel hull. But I have included a few general remarks on layout, because it is a subject about which I feel strongly. Many designers seem to produce their layouts on the basis of cramming at least six berths into anything over 20 feet! And this often produces a boat that is not suitable for anything.

Layout

I deliberately didn't include any accommodation plans in Chapter 6 on selecting designs, because it is very easy to be put off an otherwise attractive boat by an unappealing inside layout. And these layouts can be very easily altered to suit the personal taste of an owner. META have a good idea with their plans. Two or three suggested layouts are given with an additional plan consisting of just a bare outline of the boat with bulkheads fitted. Together with this plan is a page full of furniture and fittings, all drawn to scale. These can then be

Fig 54 Defer: Interior layout.

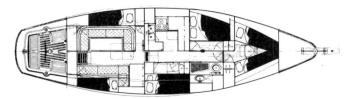

Fig 55 Endurance 44: Interior layout.

cut out and juggled into the accommodation plan until an appealing arrangement is found.

I have included some general arrangements which appeal to me, with a plan of our own layout on *Abraxis*. This latter is the Mark Three version, Marks One and Two having been scrapped after we had lived with them awhile. The ease with which we have twice drastically altered the interior layout illustrate another of the many advantages of steel construction.

In the matter of layout, I confess that I have indulged my own special interest—that of boats to be used as voyaging homes. But many of the ideas could be useful to the weekend cruising yacht too, and the technical aspects of fitting out will of course remain the same. Accommodation for permanent life aboard requires special considerations to prevent the inevitable lack of space from getting on your nerves. The most important feature is that there should be separate areas for living, cooking, sleeping and navigating. None of these

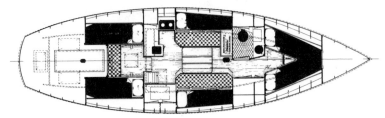

Fig 56 Al Mason 44: Interior layout.

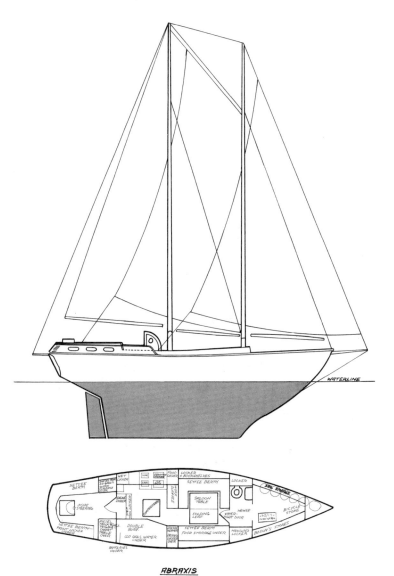

ABRAXIS

Fig 57 *Abraxis*: Profile and Interior layout.

203

should impinge on any of the others or you will find life becomes very chaotic. In this respect there is nothing worse than dual-purpose features, such as the saloon table that converts to a double bunk. We had this idea at first, but the result was that we ended up with no saloon table except when we had visitors! You can get away with these dual-purpose ideas in a weekend cruising boat because you are not aboard long enough for them to annoy you. But there is no place for them in a cruising home, as you normally have no need for the extra bunks they are designed to create. Even in the family cruiser do you really need all the bunks that boat salesmen seem to believe are necessary? Wouldn't a more comfortable layout be better?

Most boats, even cruising homes, spend the greater part of their lives in harbour, so you need to make yourself comfortable there as well as at sea. In this connection, a good-sized saloon table is well worth having—somewhere to spread yourself out for such things as writing, repairing odds and ends, or planning the next passage. And I reckon that a good-sized double bunk is another necessary requirement for a happy home! Many people condemn them out of hand as 'no good at sea', but we can just block off half with a bunk board and use that. In any case we usually try to keep out of the 'bedroom' at sea so we have a nice snug bunk to jump into when we reach port.

Two watertight bulkheads are built into our design and these have a number of advantages. Apart from the obvious benefit of preventing the spread of fire and flood (we have experienced the former but not the latter) they effectively section off from the sea cabin the noise and fumes of the engine. Additionally they give separate cabins which make for privacy if there are several people aboard (e.g. charterers).

The sequence of fitting out will be roughly as it appears in this chapter. But one word of warning. Make sure you have somewhere to feed 8ft. × 4ft. sheets of ply into the hull. I have seen even experienced builders fall into the trap of welding up the decks so that the only means of access is a 2-foot square hatch. A plate only tacked in position, a plate left out between portholes, or the removable cockpit floor over the engine, all will serve the purpose. But make sure that somewhere there is a hole big enough for the ply.

Tankage

The first thing that should be considered is tankage, as this will affect the next step which is the ballast. For living on board, the maximum amount of fuel and water should be carried consistent with the problem of weight. We carry 120 gal. of water and 150 gal. of diesel. The diesel capacity may be a bit excessive as it gives us a theoretical range of 2000 miles under power, but the water I would regard as a minimum. The tanks should be fitted as low down in the hull as possible, and it is normally preferable to keep them as near to amidships as possible in order to keep weight out of the ends. I prefer to split the water tanks so that pollution or leakage in one does not affect the entire supply. To that end our water supply is split into three separate tanks with interconnecting pipes for filling but separate demand systems. The diesel supply is split into two tanks for the same reason.

I prefer to use the ship's hull as part of the tank. In my opinion this is better than separate tanks, which can make some of the hull plating inaccessible, and a likely rust trap. Best is to build the tanks into the keel as suggested in Chapter 8. And if this is done, it is a good idea to separate the diesel and the water by a ballast compartment. If there is a choice between putting water or diesel down the keel, choose the water as this is marginally heavier (10 lb./gal, as compared with 8 lb./gal.). And this should avoid the necessity for a diesel lift pump to supply the injector pump: one less thing to go wrong.

One disadvantage of integral tanks is the risk of pollution in the event of damage or seepage at seams. But this shouldn't be a problem if the tanks are made as several units. And the integral tanks could even stop you sinking!

If you do go for separate tanks a cheap and quick approach is to buy domestic water tanks. In England these are available in 14 or 16 gauge galvanized mild steel in standard sizes of 10-gallon increments. The tanks come open-topped, but with a flange that is ideal for bolting on a lid. The cost of the tank is only a little more than the material cost.

Protection is needed inside both diesel and water tanks. While diesel oil is an extremely good protection for steel, the inside of the tank should still be protected, because condensation can form as the tank empties and this can corrode unprotected metal. Epoxy paints will give good protection but avoid any bitumen-based paints as diesel is a solvent for bitumen. For water tanks, International's water tank black works well, but make sure you let it dry thoroughly before bolting on the lid. We didn't and we were unable to get rid of its taste until we did the job again. Cement wash is a treatment which can be successful, but the right cement and the right application are essential to avoid a lime taste which is very difficult to remove. (See E. Hiscock, *Sou' West in 'Wanderer IV'*, for a story of problems of this kind.)

Cabin Soles

Cement properly applied is probably one of the best protections for bare steel. I have chipped away 30-year old concrete to reveal perfect plating. And there is the additional advantage that cement can (and must) be applied wet to the steel so that there is no problem of scrupulously drying areas as would be necessary for painting. Our bilges and ballast are cemented, and this seems highly satisfactory as a cheap and effective sole can be obtained by simply concreting to the height required and putting a carpet over the top! More sophisticated is to lay wooden flooring on the concrete and this can look very smart. It obviously scores over the carpet which you will have to take up when you go to sea. Nevertheless special concrete paint can be obtained and this doesn't look too bad.

There are several choices for a wooden sole. Decking ply, especially in teak, looks very good in fairly small areas and we have had very good service out of ours in the galley. This sort of plywood is expensive but can sometimes be obtained cheaply from the factory if a bit damaged or watermarked. Short lengths of iroko battening can often be obtained from household suppliers. Designed for flooring in houses, these battens make an excellent cabin sole. However, beware the sort of parquet flooring that comes in packets and is stuck on to a felt backing. We put this down in a galley initially but a wet passage across to Holland lifted most of the wood away from the backing and it was a hopeless mess. Lino tiles can be stuck to the concrete and this is a quick and very cheap way to do an area that is likely to be covered with a carpet in port anyway. It is best to use the non-sticky type with your own glue, as the pre-coated adhesive is easily affected by diesel and sea water, causing it to peel away. One other alternative is to just lay lino down, cut to shape.

Insulation
There is a great deal of conjecture about the need for insulation. My own experience is that an air gap between wood ceilings and the hull plating is sufficient insulation in itself, to keep the interior both warm in winter and cool in summer. And in general steel boats seem to achieve this every bit as well as their wood or GRP counterparts. As is noted by the Van de Wieles of their steel ketch *Omoo*, cabin temperatures in wooden boats in hot weather can be quite a few degrees higher than in a well insulated steel boat (see *The West in My Eyes*—A. Van de Wiele).

However if panelling is used by itself, condensation can form behind. This should not really matter, provided frames do not trap the water, and provided the hull is well painted. In any event condensation can be easily eliminated with anti-condensation paint, such as International Corkon or Blake's anti-condensation emulsion.

If you do decide to use insulation, it is important to use the right sort. I would avoid polystyrene, as even the so-called fire-resistant types burn very easily and produce a highly toxic black smoke in so doing. We had a serious fire on board because of this, and I subsequently ripped out what remained and substituted fire-proofed fibreglass loft insulation instead. But the polystyrene has the advantage that it doesn't soak up water. Water-soaked glass fibre makes a very effective rust trap. So if you do go for polystyrene, test the type you buy to make perfectly sure that it is self-extinguishing. The polystyrene bubbles in the self-extinguishing variety are filled with carbon dioxide, and this helps to damp down any flame. But the polystyrene will still burn if a flame is continuously applied to it.

By far the best insulation is a two-part expanded polyurethane foam. This is bonded directly to the hull, where it sticks as well as any glue. It not only provides extremely effective insulation but also gives total and indefinite protection to the steel. It is expensive, but the long-term benefits are enormous. In England it is obtainable from Strand Glass.

Panelling and Deckheads

Prior to fitting the hull panelling and deckhead, make sure all the wiring and plumbing has been installed, as it makes the job twice as long if it has to be done afterwards. In addition it is best if all the deck fittings are welded on prior to the cladding going up, as pulling it down again in the way of a weld is extremely tedious.

It is best to put the hull panelling up before the deckhead

as any slight gap at the join will not be noticed by the eye looking on a level with the join, and will only be noticed when looking straight up at it—such as when lying in bunk doing a 'deckhead survey'!

In order to fasten the cladding to the hull and deckhead it will first be necessary to fasten battens to the frames unless the latter are welded in such a fashion that self-tapping screws can be used to secure cladding directly to the web. (I find this latter system much slower.) Inch-square wooden battens can be simply secured to the frames by $\frac{3}{4}$in. steel (not brass!) screws secured through holes drilled in the frames. The choice of cladding material is large:

1 Varnished plywood is suitable but can look very dreary in large areas. So it is necessary to break it up by trim. But even with plenty of luxury trim, Eric Hiscock found it necessary to paint white several of the varnished panels in *Wanderer IV* to brighten up the cabin. Plywood can be quite tricky to fit without gaps if it has to be spiled on all four sides, but it has the advantage that it can be fitted in removable panels for ready access to the plate behind. I prefer matt varnish to the glossy sort—it seems to me to look more tasteful!

2 Tongue and groove is very simple and fast to fit, as the pieces you are dealing with are quite small. And it can be relatively cheap. It is available in a variety of different woods, with beech particularly attractive, but easily bruised. Pine is probably as good as any and is normally the cheapest. And, in any event, ordinary pine can be made to look sumptuous by staining a deep mahogany such as in the main saloon of the Thames sailing barge *Xylonite*.

3 Formica (and similar laminates) can be used on thin plywood to make excellent deckheads which are easy to clean, look attractive and reflect light well. White for-

mica does, however, have to be split up with wooden battens to avoid looking too stark, but these can be used to cover the joins. Matt Formica looks a lot nicer than the glossy sort, and if scratched can be made to look as good as new by rubbing down with very fine wet and dry abrasive paper used wet (unlike glossy Formica which, once damaged, is ruined for ever).

4 Treated cork tiles can make attractive cladding when stuck on thin plywood.

5 Plywood covered with certain types of vinyl cloth can be made to look quite sumptuous when fitted in panels retained in place by screws in brass cup washers.

Furniture

With your cladding in position you can build in the furniture. This is another area where steel scores, as furniture can be built in very strongly by welding up the framework in angle bar and simply screwing plywood to the bars with self-tapping screws. The structures should of course be welded in before all the painting and cladding commences, but afterthoughts are possible. We have made two changes of layout simply, cheaply and quickly by cutting out the old framework and welding in new. Remember not to fit the framework until the boat is ballasted properly, as framework fitted while she is a bit out of trim can result in bunks which slope down towards your head and an oven that produces lop-sided cakes!

Portholes

Portholes can be difficult to fit in any boat, but particularly so in steel. Ready-made versions are plentiful, but extremely expensive, and in many cases not designed with steel construction in mind. In a steel boat, there will be a gap between the panelling and the hull sides. This gap will have to be filled by an appropriate porthole design, and most proprietary

53 Rectangular portholes with rounded corners, as in *Abraxis*.

portholes do not allow for this. So the best idea is to make your own, and the possible variations are limited only by your ingenuity.

Porthole shape is critical to the look of the boat, so it is well worth making up cardboard patterns and offering them up to the hull so as to see the effect. I prefer rectangular portholes with the corners rounded, as you may see from the photograph of *Abraxis*. Our approach was for cheapness and speed, but it did work well. We cut holes to the appropriate shape in our after cabin sides, and then bolted ½in. Perspex (known under the trade-name of Plexiglass in the USA) on the inside. The bolts were countersunk into the plate and filled over with epoxy putty, so that they don't show from the outside. We used stainless bolts, but I think mild steel would do if you coat them plentifully with something like pitch. Our cladding (plywood with decorative cork finish) was screwed to wooden battens which were in turn screwed to the frames. We cut holes in the cladding to match up with the portholes, and then were left with a gap to fill between the ply and Perspex. To do this job we used offcuts of ply cut so they overlapped the window an inch and a half all the way around. And then we cut out the shape of the porthole in these pieces of ply. We then laminated them together until there was sufficient thickness to fill the gap between cladding and window. We then screwed these mock frames to the back of the ply and faired them in with more epoxy filler. We painted the frames white, but if you use offcuts of real tree wood, you could varnish them instead.

A more sophisticated alternative is to use thin (3mm.) flat bar the width of the gap between porthole and cladding and bend to shape using the porthole itself as a jig. A flange around the inside edge can be used to retain the Perspex when pushed in from the outside. The Perspex can be fixed in place with epoxy glue or through-bolted (I prefer glue). But it is obviously best to weld up the whole frame to the hull before you fit the Perspex. You can secure the cladding to the porthole frame, either by lugs welded to the frame or by battens screwed around it. Insetting the portholes in this way not only looks professional, but it also helps to protect them from damage. If this technique is used, toughened glass can be substituted for Perspex. Glass is far more satisfactory as it is not prone to surface scratching and crazing in the same way as Perspex.

Finally, a quick and easy system is to through-bolt Perspex on to the outside of the plating. While marginally acceptable for coach roofs, I don't like the system for flush-deckers as the portholes can be very vulnerable.

Financial circumstances dictated that we had to live on board while fitting out, but if it is at all possible this is best avoided. We were forever moving gear backwards and forwards from one end of the boat to the other in order to get at a particular job. At worst try and get a store nearby ashore where loose gear can be safely left. However, there is one advantage to living amidst all the wood shavings and paint fumes—it is a real incentive to getting the job done quickly.

14

Machinery and Steering

Steering

The first choice to be made is *inboard* or *outboard* rudder. Although this will be dictated by the design, a few words about the relative merits are appropriate here. It is generally held that the inboard version is harder to fit because of the difficulty of making it watertight, but this problem is of little consequence in a steel boat. However, the internal rudder post can seriously impinge on accommodation, especially if the boat has an after cabin, and can make the rudder difficult to remove should repairs be necessary. Arguments against the outboard rudder centre on its susceptibility to damage in crowded harbours or in heavy following seas, with some people additionally claiming that it is aesthetically less pleasing. And another problem is the difficulty of fitting standard wind-vane steering systems. Nevertheless, ease of construction and repair makes an outboard fitting the one for me. (See photo 55 of *Vega*'s rudder with trim tab for self-steering attached, and tubular bumkin acting as protection.)

If an inboard rudder is called for in the design, it will probably be made watertight by a rudder tube extending up above the waterline and welded to the hull plating (Fig. 58). If the tube is made to go well above the waterline no capping will be necessary to keep the water out. But if not, then bearings and gland packing can be used as an alternative, as in Fig. 59. Tufnol or similar is better for this purpose than a straightforward metal bearing which will not last long especially under water. The tube itself should be made out of

54   Semi-balanced rudders are unsuitable for sailing boats.

as thick a section as possible, as wastage is inevitable over a period of time. The tube should be galvanized, but even so the proximity to the propeller and difficulty of painting inside can result in a limited life through electrolysis. But this is not a major problem. The rudder tube on *Abraxis* was eaten away paper thin when we acquired her, but that after many years. And the job of replacing only took an afternoon.

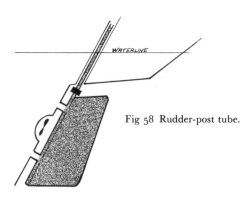

WATERLINE

Fig 58 Rudder-post tube.

214

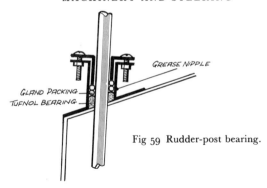

Fig 59 Rudder-post bearing.

The rudder post itself should be made out of solid round bar of at least 30mm. diameter, to take the considerable strain and give plenty of margin for corrosion. But if this bar goes straight up through the tube to the stock, then there will be a problem in removing it for damage repair. The boat will have to be jacked up sufficiently high for the entire post and rudder to be dropped down and out through the tube, or dropped down while afloat. Neither option is a good one, so for this reason rudders are sometimes bolted to the post with flanges as in Fig. 60. This is not entirely satisfactory as the

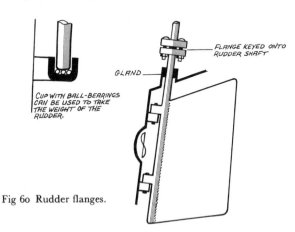

Fig 60 Rudder flanges.

bolts will corrode, causing a weak point, considerable drag-forming turbulence will be created, and the join will look ugly if it appears above the waterline. Another option is to join just inside the boat, with a bearing to keep out the water, but this is a potential leak. Our choice on *Abraxis* was a solid post which would need to be cut to remove the rudder, although most repairs can be done *in situ*. However, we did make sure that the prop shaft would come out past the rudder and that the propeller could be taken off without rudder removal. We achieved this by having the rudder tube of internal diameter sufficient to enable the post to be manoeuvred to allow clearance. But in certain types of installation, even this may not allow propeller removal, so a section may need to be cut out of the rudder as in Fig. 61: this should not result in a weakness because of the inherent strength of the steel, but could result in reduced efficiency.

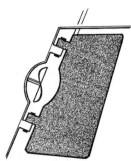

Fig 61 Section of rudder cut out to allow propeller shaft removal.

As to the type of rudder itself, this will depend largely on the type of boat. But it is worth making the general comment that semi-balanced rudders with the usual accompanying large propeller aperture, while OK in power craft, are not suitable for a sailing boat (photo 54). They create drag and can destroy the feel essential for a sailing boat's helm. (See E. Hiscock, *Sou' West in 'Wanderer IV'*). Rudders can be cut out of

55   *Vega*'s rudder with trim tab for self-steering,
and protective bumkin.

flat plate, or made up hollow. Weight for weight the made-up
version will be stronger and arguably more hydrodynamic
than flat plate, so this would be my choice. For a hollow
rudder, 3mm. plate should be amply thick and sometimes
even less is used, whereas at least 7mm. is necessary if the
rudder is of solid plate. Fabricating the hollow rudder should
be little more difficult than cutting out of flat plate. And the
join to the rudder post can be stronger because of less weld
concentration. Fig. 63 illustrates different methods of welding the post to the rudder.

217

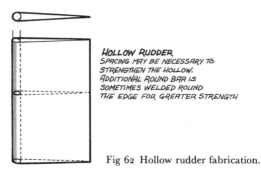

HOLLOW RUDDER
SPACING MAY BE NECESSARY TO
STRENGTHEN THE HOLLOW.
ADDITIONAL ROUND BAR IS
SOMETIMES WELDED ROUND
THE EDGE FOR GREATER STRENGTH

Fig 62 Hollow rudder fabrication.

It is often asserted that the thin plate used in hollow rudders can be subject to corrosion, especially from the inside. But the plate will only corrode from the inside while there is oxygen, and this will quickly be consumed as the steel oxidizes. Once this has happened there should be no further wastage, and it will only recommence if a weld fails. But in any event the whole problem can be virtually eliminated by having the entire rudder hot-dip galvanized before it is installed. An easy, cheap and worthwhile task, and then the rudder should well outlast the rest of the boat. For the purpose of

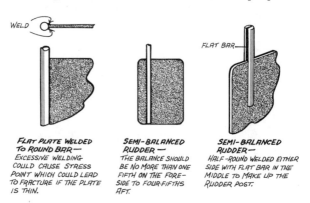

WELD

FLAT BAR

**FLAT PLATE WELDED
TO ROUND BAR—**
EXCESSIVE WELDING
COULD CAUSE STRESS
POINT WHICH COULD LEAD
TO FRACTURE IF THE PLATE
IS THIN.

**SEMI-BALANCED
RUDDER —**
THE BALANCE SHOULD
BE NO MORE THAN ONE
FIFTH ON THE FORE–
SIDE TO FOUR-FIFTHS
AFT.

**SEMI-BALANCED
RUDDER—**
HALF-ROUND WELDED EITHER
SIDE WITH FLAT BAR IN THE
MIDDLE TO MAKE UP THE
RUDDER POST.

Fig 63 Welding rudder-post to rudder.

galvanizing, holes (minimum half-inch) will need to be drilled in the rudder, to let the zinc inside and to prevent the
assembly exploding in the hot zinc bath. This hole can be
plugged after galvanizing is complete. And as a belt and
braces approach, the hollow rudder could be filled with oil
via the hole to further prevent interior corrosion. Alternatively the rudder could be protected by oil in this way without
the galvanizing.

Attaching the rudder to the boat is the next task, and this
will normally be achieved using the pintle and gudgeon
method. Although these are sometimes welded straight on to
the keel and rudder, a better scheme is to have them solidly
bolted through. This enables their easy removal for building
up when the constant wear has made them sloppy. Solidly

56 Pintle and gudgeon rudder attachment; sometimes welded, but
better through-bolted.

bolting pintles to the thin plate of a hollow rudder can be difficult as the bolt holes can tend to enlarge with wear. So a compromise is to have just the gudgeon removable from the keel, which will probably be of thicker plate. However, it is possible to take out excessive wear with everything *in situ*, by cutting in half pipe of approximate size to fit the pintle and then welding this into the gudgeon.

Plastic bearings can be obtained from, amongst others, META in France, and their use will avoid direct metal to metal contact which has but a short life.

Some power boats have short spade rudders unsupported below the waterline, but this does not seem to be satisfactory. If a keel is not available to act as support, it is probably better to weld up a bar skeg which can also be used as support for the propeller tube. This can have the additional advantage of giving some protection to the rudder and propeller against the attacks of loose lengths of rope, plastic bags and the like.

If the boat is to be steered by tiller, few further construction problems arise. But most boats over about 35 feet tend to

57 A spade rudder.

THE SKEG BAR GIVES SOME SUPPORT
AND PROTECTION TO THE RUDDER
AND PROPELLER SHAFT TUBE.

Fig 64 Skeg bar.

be fitted with wheel steering, and with a centre cockpit this will usually be unavoidable. There are several possible ways of connecting up the wheel and the following are some examples:

Worm drive
Quadrant and wire
Hydraulic
Cable

Worm Drive
A good old-fashioned system this one (see photo 58 of worm gear on the steel Thames barge *Xylonite*). However, although

58 Worm gear for steering on Thames barge *Xylonite*.

59 A worm and peg gearbox for steering.

their robustness and virtual infallibility make worm drives ideal if you are fitting out an ex-trader, most of the versions to be found are much too big and cumbersome for consideration aboard a yacht.

A more compact and equally satisfactory alternative is a worm and peg gearbox that can be mounted straight on to the rudder shaft and powered by direct rod linkage to the steering wheel. Such boxes can often be obtained very cheaply from lorry breakers and an example is featured in photo 59. Some form of universal joint will be required at the input side, as it will seldom be possible to line up the gearbox shaft exactly so that the drive rod goes at right angles to the wheel. Again the scrapyard can come to our rescue, as the universal joints on front-wheel-drive cars (e.g. Austin 1100) will serve excellently for our purpose. (Again see photograph.) On *Abraxis* the gearbox was made to serve both an inside and an outside steering position, by brazing a second input shaft on to the aft side of the worm.

The worm in a worm and peg gearbox cannot be turned from the rudder end, and therefore does not transmit much 'feel' back to the wheel. But we have not found this to be a significant problem in practice. Non-reversibility can, in fact, have its advantages when it comes to leaving the helm unattended. However, I would not recommend the system for a racer.

You will need to check that the gearbox you buy has sufficient reduction for the job. The maximum angle from centreline at which the rudder is reckoned to be still effective is 34 degrees i.e. 68 degrees from lock to lock. Two turns of the wheel from lock to lock is normally the minimum considered sufficient to allow for fine adjustment of course. Accordingly the gearbox will have to provide a reduction of $(360° + 360°)/68°$ or approximately 10:1.

Quadrant
Perhaps the most common type of steering system is quadrant drive on the rudder shaft which is connected to the wheel

60   Quadrant for steering.

by wires. It is certainly cheap. The quadrant pictured in photo 60 is a cast version, but one could easily be made up from bits of steel. The arc of the quadrant should be kept a fraction smaller than that of the rudder (i.e. a bit less than 68 degrees), as this will ensure that the rudder can't be pulled hard over against its stops.

The number of turns, lock to lock, will be dictated by how the wire is connected to the wheel. The two main methods are sprockets or a drum. The first way uses motor-bicycle chain connected into the wire by shackles, and passing over a sprocket attached to the wheel. The alternative is a drum with the wire wrapped around it; at least four turns to get sufficient grip. This latter system will call for greater tension in the wire, although both methods will call for some way of taking up slack, and it is normal to put a rigging screw into the wire on either side of the quadrant for this purpose. The drum or sprocket diameter will dictate the number of turns required to move the rudder from lock to lock—the bigger the diameter, the fewer turns. To calculate the appropriate size accurately, measure along the arc of the quadrant. This length will then be the circumference of drum to necessitate one turn lock to lock. As three turns are normally about right, divide the arc length by three. To turn this circumference into diameter, use the formula $D = C/\pi$ ($\pi = 3 \cdot 142$). If the

61 and 62   Drum steering on *Joshua*.

sprocket option is chosen, remember to measure the diameter to the inside of the sprockets. Simpson Lawrence (and others) market all the components for such a system, but they can all be made up very readily with the welder. The main items I would buy would be special plastic pulleys for wire leads. (See photos 61 and 62 of drum steering on *Joshua* for an illustration of how simple this method can be.)

Hydraulic Steering

Hydraulic steering is often found on larger craft and especially in motor boats, but it is not well suited to sailing boats as no feel is transmitted back from the rudder. The hydraulics give effortless power and there is the additional advantage that the pipes can be led along much more tortuous angles than either rod or wire linkages. A hydraulic system is normally fairly reliable, but the initial cost is very high. However, such a system might be the only answer where it proves impossible to arrange an appropriate lead for wires or rods. Among others, W. H. den Ouden in Schiedam, Holland (British Agents, A. N. Wallis), market systems suitable for most boats.

225

Cable Steering

Another possibility is a cable steering system, such as the ones marketed in England, by Teleflex/Morse. Quite commonly fitted to small runabout craft, cable steering can also be obtained in sizes suitable for relatively large boats. But the cost is high.

Rod and wire are the cheapest, and perhaps the most reliable. I would opt for one of these and find ways of overcoming the possible impingement on accommodation. But whatever form of wheel steering you choose, it's normal to have some sort of fall-back *tiller* device as well. On an inboard system, this is commonly achieved by continuing the rudder post up through the deck with a square drive at the top of the post to take a tiller. With an outboard rudder it is common to have a permanent tiller fitted as an alternative form of steering, or sometimes the wire drive from the wheel is linked direct to a tiller, instead of to the quadrant.

It is a common practice among ocean voyagers to drill a hole in the top of the rudder itself, to take a shackle. (In a hollow rudder watertightness can still be achieved by welding a tube between the two holes.) In the event of total steering breakdown, a shackle can be fitted and ropes down from either side of the boat used to give a temporary but effective means of control—provided the rudder hasn't dropped off as well!

Engines

It is often advocated that engines should be fitted almost as soon as the hull is complete on the grounds that access will be the easiest at this stage. While there is a lot of sense in this, there is always the danger that you might ignore the engine in subsequent fitting out and end up with it stuck in the boat for life. It will need to come out sooner or later, so it is best to make sure that hatches are large enough to allow for this, and that surrounding woodwork isn't made too permanent.

Engine Installation

The engine is best installed over ballast rather than tanks, as the tanks will need to be accessible for periodic inspection and cleaning. The ballast will need to be plated over to protect it from water and oil drips from the engine; bilge water down inside ballast is impossible to remove and could lead to electrolysis.

Bear in mind accessibility. The tendency in modern yachts is to install the engine so that it impinges the least on accommodation. This follows from the apparent need to cram as many berths as possible into the tiniest of boats. The net result is that the engine becomes difficult to work on, jeopardizing regular maintenance. Accordingly access should be to all four sides, and I like to have a built-in method of hoisting the engine out. On our boat, an eye flange is permanently welded directly above the engine. And a tackle led down to a pulley and up through the hatch to the main halyard lifts the engine out effortlessly.

While a separate walk-in engine room with steel bulkheads and steel watertight doors to contain fire, flood and fumes, is a highly desirable feature, this is difficult to achieve on anything much under 50 feet. However, asbestos-sandwiched plywood makes a good fire retainer and serves as a sound barrier as well. (Take care to avoid breathing asbestos dust when working with the blue sort, because of the danger of asbestosis.) Our engine cover is made like this and all parts can be readily dismantled for all-round access. One of our watertight bulkheads is on the aft side of our engine, and the forward accommodation is protected from migrating bilgewater by a partial bulkhead and a large sump.

It follows from my comments on accessibility that I don't much like engines fitted down in the keel. They can be almost impossible to work on, although it has to be admitted that there is an advantage in terms of keeping weight down low.

Engine installation on some shallow-draft boats is often extremely difficult because of the impossibility of getting the engine low enough without encroaching on the accommodation, but Volvo Penta have recently introduced an angle drive that can sometimes solve the problem.

Or how about considering belt-drive instead of the conventional gearbox? Both these methods allow the engine to be installed in the often wasted space towards the stern of the boat. Yet another possibility is hydraulic drive, which allows the engine to be sited anywhere in the boat. The cost is little higher than that of the gearbox it replaces.

The engine bearers themselves should be made as long as possible to spread the load. While this is nowhere near so important on little boats as it is on ships, engine vibration over a period of time could weaken welds on short bearers and lead to ultimate failure. And short bearers can place undue strain on a small part of the hull fabric. For similar reasons, it is best to avoid welding the bearers directly to the hull plating, as attaching to the frames further spreads the load. It can be quite tricky to get the bearers at exactly the right height. Too high is a disaster, as they will have to be cut out and the job done again. (See E. Hiscock's problems in *Sou' West in 'Wanderer IV'*.) Too low can be coped with by using packing pieces, but not if they are very low. The only real answer is to fit the stern gear first, and then with the engine suspended in position, tack weld the bearers into place. Alternatively, an engine mock-up can be used, but it will have to be very accurate.

I would recommend flexible rubber mountings, together with a flexible propeller-shaft coupling. These can do much to reduce the drumming and noise transmission that can sometimes occur in a steel hull. And there is also the advantage that slight inaccuracies in alignment will not be quite so serious as in a rigid installation. Another advantage is that most flexible couplings are designed to shear under a shock load, thereby saving the gearbox from damage (but carry a spare set of rubber coupling doughnuts). But the biggest plus is the fact that the mounts and coupling can electrically isolate the engine from the hull, thereby reducing the risk of electrolysis.

The fitting of the engine itself is really outside the scope of this book, as my stated intention is to deal only with those aspects of fitting-out as are specific to steel, and to leave other matters to the myriad of specialist fitting-out books. Nevertheless engine installation is critical. So I am going to include some straightforward ideas on layout which can perhaps prevent the usual mistakes, that can be both expensive and dangerous.

Engine Ancillaries

I work on the premise that if you are going to have an engine aboard, it has got to be reliable. Better none at all than one that fails to start when you are relying on it. I also believe that an oil (diesel) engine is a must. With the modern light-weight diesels that are available, there can be little justification for fitting a petrol version. Petrol engines are expensive to run, unreliable, relatively short-lived, and above all petrol fumes are highly dangerous in the confines of a small boat. With an oil engine in good condition (and even one in very bad condition) you need only to make sure fuel and air are getting to the engine, and that the exhaust is getting away, and the thing must run. Hence every effort must be made to ensure that these parts of the system work and keep working.

Fuel tanks can usefully be installed slightly above the level of the engine, so that the fuel feeds in by gravity. If not, there may be a need to raise the fuel by a lift pump in addition to the fuel injection pump, and that gives one more thing to go wrong. I prefer to install at least two separate tanks so that if one tank is contaminated, then you don't lose the whole supply. Also the tanks should have ready access for examination and cleaning out sludge periodically. This can be achieved by having a hole cut in the top or side with a plate that bolts over the top. Best to make the hole at least the width of your shoulders so you can really get inside to give it a good clean. But I prefer to have the whole tank top removable, and this is in many respects easier to construct. Simply weld up the tank without a top, then weld flat bar around the edge. Now cut out plate for a lid. With the lid in place (perhaps lightly tacked to prevent it moving) drill holes all around the edge at no more than 2in. intervals to take a $\frac{3}{16}$in. bolt. Now remove the lid and poke the bolts up through the flat bar from below, and weld in place. You can now bolt the lid on after sealing with a gasket or silicone rubber (ordinary rubber will not do as it will be destroyed by the diesel). But just a final word before you bolt it up solid. If it is a big tank, then it will need baffles to stop the oil slurping around inside as the ship rolls. I prefer baffles every 18 inches or so, and they should be welded to the sides leaving a gap top and bottom. Don't do without them for a quick job. You will regret it when you are trying to get some sleep to the accompaniment of a loud slopping in your ear.

The tanks will need a stop-cock each, to cut off the fuel should that be necessary, and they will also need a means of draining. This latter is best suited below the take-off point for the supply to the engine, so that periodically the sludgy oil at the bottom can be drained off. The pipes themselves should be metal not plastic as an obvious fire precaution, and theoretically they should be of steel and not copper, as the latter reacts with diesel to the detriment of the pipe. But we have copper pipe and have had no trouble. So I would risk them, rather than the steel which can corrode from the outside. Keep a look-out, though, for possible fractures. Also important, is to secure the pipes solidly to guard against fracture through vibration. And it is necessary to provide some means of absorbing vibration where the pipe leaves the engine and joins the tank. One way is to have a steel walled flexible pipe (but make sure it is suitable for diesel); an alternative is to bend the pipe in a spiral so that this absorbs any movement.

Exhausts can be either wet or dry, and of the two I much prefer the former. Wet exhausts are quieter, longer-lived and much less prone to fume leakage than the dry sort. Dry exhausts need means of absorbing the vibration at the engine end, and this will normally consist of a piece of flexible steel exhaust welded into the solid exhaust pipe. The flexible can be obtained in either stainless or mild steel, with the stainless being a lot better bet (but see Chapter 4 for the special rods to weld stainless to mild steel). Mild steel flexible pipe seems very prone to corrosion, and has a very short life. It is also prone to leak fumes even when new. And it can fracture through vibration.

If sea-water cooling is used, then the cooling water can be fed into the exhaust pipe thus cooling the exhaust, and enabling rubber exhaust hose to be used. The rubber absorbs vibration, should be totally fume proof and does a lot to deaden noise. But correct installation is critical to avoid the potential disaster of cooling water back in the engine. And this is particularly a problem where the engine is installed below the waterline.

When the engine is running, the cooling water will be blown out of the pipe by the exhaust fumes. But when it stops, water can filter back down into the engine. As some of the valves will inevitably be open, the water will get into the bores, where it can do irreparable harm. Several precautions have to be taken. There should be an elbow at the exhaust manifold to prevent water running back into the engine, and the water inlet should be angled away from the engine. (The elbow must be metal as it will not be water-cooled.) It is useful next to incorporate a water trap into the system to catch the unexhausted water which will run back when the engine is stopped. Another necessary feature is a swan neck in the system, with the pipe carried up above the waterline and then back down again in order to prevent sea water being forced into the system by wave action at the outlet end.

With engines fitted below the waterline, there is the risk of water forcing its way past the water pump impeller and into the exhaust system with the engine stationary. Water can then build up in the system, until it overflows the trap and filters back into the engine. One way to prevent this is to carry the spent water pipe from the engine well up above the waterline and down again before injecting it into the exhaust pipe. Accordingly if water is forced past the impeller, it won't go above the waterline and won't, therefore, be able to reach the exhaust system. Another safeguard is to put a vent in the spent water pipe to prevent this siphon effect.

One further precaution is to turn the inlet water seacock off a few seconds before stopping the engine. This shouldn't really be necessary if all the previous safeguards are observed, and it can damage rubber impellers if the engine is allowed to run for too long dry. It is useful to up the revs for a few seconds before stopping to help blast the water out. If on the other hand the engine is allowed to idle for a long time before it is stopped, this can lead to a build up of spent water in the system which can then filter back into the bores.

If this does happen, it need not be too disastrous provided that it is discovered quickly enough. (If it is left for a long time the whole engine could seize solid.) You can discover the water through emulsified oil and a high level on the dipstick or by oil seepage around the joints. The dipstick can usefully be checked every time the engine is run, but if you don't discover it before you try to turn the engine, you will quickly discover it then. The engine will normally be impossible to turn, because of the water in the bores. If this is the case stop trying instantly or you will cause severe damage by trying to compress the water. The answer is to open the decompressors, and to slowly turn the engine over, preferably by hand. The water should then be forced out via the valve holes which are held open by the decompressors. A few turns should get rid of most of the water. But if water has got into the sump, you will need to drain the oil, change the filter and flush through with several lots of clean oil before further use.

Heat Exchangers

Many modern diesel installations call for freshwater cooling with heat exchangers, and this will definitely be the case if an automobile engine conversion is being used. Steel boats can score here, as it is often possible to use the hull itself as the heat exchanger. A fresh-water tank in the keel may be all that is necessary with the cooling water drawn from one end at the bottom and the hot water from the engine fed back in at the top. The heat from this closed circuit system will then be dissipated through the hull plating, cooled by the sea water passing outside. The greater the area of plating, the more effective this system will be, so tanks should be as long as possible. Neat and simple, but remember to leave access to the tank for periodic de-scaling. The system can also be used to provide hot water for the galley, proved there is a means of replenishing the water as it is used.

An alternative system, often encountered on work boats, is to pipe the cooling water through tubes actually welded to the outside of the hull. This gives a large area over which the heat can be dissipated, but in my view the method is unsatisfactory as the pipes are very susceptible to damage, especially on slipping. This in turn could result in unseen damage to the engine, through pollution of the cooling water by salt.

Electrics

With the fuel supply and the exhaust installed, the engine should now run. But electrics are useful; indeed many units require electric starting. So some comment on electrical installation is appropriate.

I would go for an all 12-volt supply. Although 24 volt has greater power for driving accessories, which will also be more robust, everything in 24 volt costs a lot more and can be difficult to obtain. Whereas in 12 volt, a lot of mass-produced car and caravan equipment can readily be adapted to work. For example, I carry two spare alternators, obtained in excellent condition from a car breaker. And the pair cost me a tenth of the likely cost of one 24-volt unit. (Check that they are negative earth.)

It is useful to split the batteries into two lots. One bank for engine starting, and the other for ship's supply. Battery sizes are quoted in amp hours which is most readily understood as the length of time a 1 amp bulb would take to completely flatten the battery. (Technically capacity is calculated on a greater draw per hour than this, and a slow draw would flatten the battery slightly more quickly than its stated capacity.) The amp hours capacity given should be regarded as a maximum, and will reduce as the battery gets older. The minimum power necessary to turn over a smallish engine is about 60 amp hours and bigger machines may need substantially greater power. The required capacity for the ship's use should be calculated as the maximum demand likely for navigation lights and domestic use for the maximum period likely between recharging, plus an inefficiency factor of up to 20 per cent. As an example, we carry three 130 amp hour batteries for the ship's supply, and one at 80 amp hours for the engine.

The two banks can usefully be interlinked for charging, and for combining battery power if the engine battery is low. But ship's supply should only come from the ship's bank or you may run down the engine battery and accordingly have no means of starting. A blocking diode, a sort of electrical one way valve, can be used to allow the charging of both banks to prevent withdrawal from the engine bank. But I don't like blocking diodes. Like all electrical equipment, they are prone to failure in the unsympathetic environment aboard a boat. And if they go wrong, you have no means of telling before your batteries are run down. In certain cases they can also damage electrical equipment if they fail. Simplest and far the best is a hand operated isolator switch. To fit such a switch, first connect all the batteries in parallel, but omit the positive lead to the engine battery. This lead can then be fitted from the engine battery to a point near the switchboard where the isolator switch can be installed. And from there the wire will be led back to the ship's battery bank.

If the alternator is connected to the engine battery it can charge that first. And when fully charged, as denoted by the ammeter, the switch can be thrown and the domestic bank charged as well. To a certain extent, it doesn't much matter whether you apply the charge to the engine's or the ship's batteries, as electricity, like water tends to flow so as to even itself out. So the charge in the engine battery will flow across the ship's batteries as soon as the switch is open. But what does matter is that you take the ship's requirements only from the ship's battery bank, and that the switch is closed except when charging. Failure to observe this could allow the engine battery to be flattened by domestic use.

All electrical fittings should be connected to a twin cable double-insulated circuit. On no account should the hull of the boat be used as the earth as in a car, as this will considerably exacerbate electrolysis. For the same reason every precaution must be taken to prevent electrical seepage, where, for example, fittings are attached to the hull. One difficult area is the engine itself. The engine will usually be earthed for starting purposes, so it must be insulated from the hull. This insulation can be readily achieved using the flexible mountings and couplings that I recommended earlier in the chapter.

Propeller Tubes and Shafts

Bronze and stainless steel shafts are commonly used in boat-building, but a case can be made against both of them for steel boats. Bronze and steel are a long way apart in the cathodic scale so electrolytic reaction between a bronze shaft and the steel hull will be almost inevitable. And if the stern tube is steel, then the problem could ultimately be serious. Nor is stainless an entirely satisfactory solution. Although it sets up less electrolysis, it is prone to shielding corrosion (see Chapter 15), and recent research has made a strong case against its use under water. Stainless steel depends upon oxygen to maintain its molecular structure. If deprived of oxygen, the rapid corrosion can result. And one way that oxygen deprivation can occur is if barnacles attach themselves under water. This can result in serious pitting and ultimate failure. There is little to choose between stainless and bronze in terms of cost, with bronze being softer and, therefore, cheaper to work. But this softness can lead to much more rapid wear, which may well make stainless more economic in the long term.

I prefer steel shafts and steel stern tubes, thereby keeping electrolysis to a minimum and incidentally cutting costs. Corrosion will still be a problem, though, because of the water which will inevitably be slopping around in this area. So every effort must be made to protect the steel. Galvanizing the shaft and tube before fitting is a good first step, and binding with fibreglass tape and resin should provide total protection (epoxy paint would do as an alternative). There is some merit in welding the coupling flange on to the shaft before galvanizing, as this can save the cost of cutting a keyway. But you won't then be able to get the shaft out without first removing the engine. If the stern tube is welded into the boat, the galvanizing will obviously be destroyed at the weld point. So it may be best to secure the tube with bolts. And this will have the additional advantage of making replacement easier, should this ever be necessary.

Galvanized steel doesn't make a good bearing surface. To overcome this problem, the shaft can be white metalled or metal sprayed (usually with some form of stainless steel) in the region of the bearings and stern gland. This process can normally be arranged through most good engineering shops, and will probably be cheaper than a stainless or bronze shaft. Bearings and glands are usually only available in bronze, so this will probably have to be used. The outboard bearing is sometimes hard rubber, sometimes all bronze, with the rubber perhaps being preferable on a steel boat from the point of view of electrolysis. The inboard bearing will provide for gland packing, and sometimes the outboard bearing will have similar provision, thereby providing two lines of defence against leaks. Provision will be required for lubricating the glands and bearings, if they are not lubricated by water. A standard grease gun can be made to serve this purpose if linked to the gland via a steel tube.

Propellers

It would be logical to use a steel propeller as nearly everything so far has been steel. But here we run into difficulties. Whereas steel tube and shaft are readily available from most stockists, steel propellers are difficult to obtain as the market is geared to bronze. A steel propeller could be made specially, but its cost would probably be in excess of that of a bronze version despite the higher price of this material. And there would probably be a considerable delay. In any event, as propellers are made by casting, a steel propeller would have a slightly different electrolytic potential than the rolled steel plate of the hull, so electrolysis problems wouldn't be completely avoided. And there is danger of electrolysis between unprotected cast propellers and bronze bearings to the detriment of the propeller. And as it is almost impossible to keep paint on propellers they are difficult to protect.

237

Stainless props are a possible alternative, and have now become only a little more expensive than bronze. But I suspect them on account of the previously discussed problems of using stainless steel underwater. So bronze may be the best answer for propellers after all. Provided local anodes are fitted in close proximity to the propeller, and the hull is kept well protected, no problems should result.

Variable-pitch propellers have much to recommend them. This book is no place for a full discussion, but their advantages include the possible avoidance of the need for a gearbox, ability to adjust pitch precisely to engine speed, and the ability to set blades fore-and-aft so as to create minimum drag when sailing.

Sumps and Pumps

The engine will need a drip tray to catch all the spots of diesel and lubricating oil that will inevitably collect. There will also need to be a sump to catch any water that comes in via the stern gland, or from elsewhere. (Not that there should be very much water aboard a steel boat. If there is, something is wrong.) In Chapter 8, I pointed out the advantages of building in the sump when making up the keel arrangement; but if this wasn't done, then a concrete version can rapidly be made. It should be deep rather than wide, as this will prevent the bilge water slopping around the plates, and will provide somewhere to locate the bilge pumps.

Commercial vessels built to Lloyd's are required to have a complex system of central bilge pumps with interconnecting pipes through to each watertight compartment. This is not desirable on a yacht. If the yacht does have watertight compartments, then it is much better and cheaper to have a separate bilge pump for each, with perhaps a portable spare. It is useful to have drain holes in the bulkheads and these will normally be fitted with bungs. If the holes are made of such a size that their water throughput can be coped with by the pumps in the adjacent compartments, then the advantages of the Lloyd's system are gained without the complexity. Our own boat has this arrangement, with electric pumps in each of the three compartments, a manual pump in the engine compartment and a manual spare. An engine-driven pump for emergencies completes the system.

Seacocks

Engines need seacocks and so normally do galleys, heads and pumps. And all these can add up to a lot of holes in the side of the boat, each of which is a potential leak that could sink her. Eric Hiscock, in a rather despairing article on the joys of *Wanderer IV*'s machinery, counted no less than eighteen of the wretched things. But I have cut ours down to six and I am still considering getting rid of a further two by resorting to the famous Herreshoff cedar bucket. Apart from the heads, our only seacock below the waterline is the sea-water cooling inlet for the engine, and that has to stay. The pump outlets are all well above the waterline (to hell with the topside paint!), but even then seacocks are essential. I didn't think so at first, and wondered why we shipped water on one tack and not on the other! Our sink outlets have long since been welded up. That job was done straight after one of their seacocks failed in a strong blow off the Lizard Head in Cornwall. A simple problem to fix, but a lot of water found its way aboard before we found the source of the leak. The sink now drains into the sump. 'Don't do it,' everyone said; 'bits of food in the bilge will smell terribly.' But we find it works well, and it is a lot better for my peace of mind. The sump is pumped out instantly after the sinks have been drained, and a dash of disinfectant keeps it smelling sweet and pure. And as for a salt water tap—well, I believe that if the water is pure enough to use for washing up, then the weather will probably be healthy enough to do the washing up on deck in the bucket anyway.

For those seacocks that are essential, the choice is between bronze, steel or plastic. (I would veto stainless on the grounds of expense, scarcity and the crevice corrosion problem.) I would choose plastic for anything well above the waterline, and bronze for anything below. Plastic, because it is tough and durable and doesn't give electrolysis problems. But I wouldn't use plastic seacocks below the waterline because fire will destroy them. So a steel boat's resistance to fire would be lost. Marginally acceptable is to use metal seacocks in the engine room and plastic elsewhere, but I would not risk it. Steel seacocks are a possibility, but their susceptibility to corrosion puts them out of the question for me, for such a vital piece of equipment. Alternatively steel standpipes can be welded into the hull so as to come up above the waterline, but even these are not the complete answer. It is difficult to protect the inside of such tubes, so they can eventually be eaten away by electrolysis. Galvanizing doesn't cure this, as the zinc is anodic, so will be eroded. Coating in pitch is probably the best bet.

On balance I would go for a bronze seacock, but I see the advantages of standpipes. The bronze can of course set up electrolysis to the detriment of the surrounding plate. And a cheap brass version could de-zincify and collapse itself. But provided the seacock is of proper bronze, and is well insulated from the steel hull when it is fitted (Jeffrey's Seamflex will do for this job), and provided the hull itself is well insulated with an epoxy paint scheme, no problems should result. As a precaution, should the paint be damaged, I additionally fit a local anode close to each of the seacocks.

15

Corrosion Protection

A well maintained steel boat will last as long, probably longer, than one made of any other material. (Our boat is 30 years old, incidentally.) And even if a substantial re-skinning is required, this is easy because of the great local strength of steel. However, with the modern protection schemes available, there is no reason why such re-skinning should ever be necessary. And a steel boat will never wear out through use and exposure to sunlight in the way that a GRP version can.

Electrolysis

Rust is traditionally thought of as the enemy of steel. But it is not the real enemy. In fact, rust is easy enough to keep in check, even with a conventional paint scheme. And the ugly rust streaks that result from chipped paint are seldom serious unless left for a long time. No, it is electrolysis that presents the real danger. Electrolytic action will occur when metals of different electrical potentials are immersed in an electrolyte such as sea water. An electric current will flow between the metals causing the decay of the least noble. And this problem will become the more acute, the warmer and more saline the water is, and the more stray electrical currents there are flying around the boat. Nor is it necessary for different metals to be present for electrolysis to occur. Because of the molecular structure of steel, especially stainless steel, varying electrical potentials will arise in different areas of the metal itself, with some areas having slightly higher negative electrical potential (anodic) relative to other areas (cathodic). Currents will flow between the anodic and the cathodic areas, to the detriment of the former. At the anodes, iron will go into solution and react in the presence of oxygen with the hydroxide at the cathodes, causing decay. This problem is worse near the waterline where the sea water is heavily saturated with oxygen giving greater corrosion potential. And this is just where the paint is subject to damage from scraping against quays etc.

Anodes

The best way to prevent electrolysis is to seal the plate from the electrolyte, i.e. to paint it. However, as the paint can be damaged, some additional protection is required. This can be achieved by fitting zinc sacrificial anodes to the hull. These anodes are less noble than steel and will be wasted away gradually and in so doing prevent the steel itself from wasting away.

Sound electrical contact of the anodes to the hull is essential, and the easiest way to ensure this is to weld studs to the hull and simply to bolt the anodes on. When the time comes for renewal, wasted anodes unbolt very easily, and bolting on a new one is the work of a few minutes between tides. As well as proper attachment, the correct positioning of these anodes is crucial. M. G. Duff (also agents worldwide) will advise on positioning and supply the anodes, but as an example, I cite the arrangement on our own boat. We have two 12in. anodes

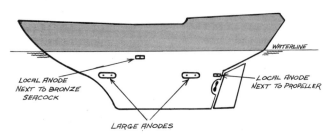

Fig 65 Anode layout.

bolted on each side of the boat at the turn of the bilge, as in Fig. 65. Additionally, there is a local anode bolted right next to each of the underwater bronze fittings—the two seacocks and the propeller.

It is only in the area of our seacocks and propeller that any serious wastage has occurred. Here we have lost up to 25 per cent of the plate thickness, and when we bought the boat, the rudder tube had wasted away to such an extent that replacement was essential. But all this had occurred through a long period of neglect, with no cathodic protection, and with virtually no underwater paint. Until we could get a sound paint scheme on the bottom, we had to rely on anodes to hold the electrolysis in check. They wasted away quite quickly (the big ones lasted about a year, the local ones about six months). But now we have an epoxy scheme, and the anodes last far longer.

From all this you might reasonably conclude that it would be wise to avoid bronze underwater fittings at all costs. But as we saw in the last chapter—they are not very easy to avoid.

One more obvious point about anodes. Make sure that no paint gets splashed on them, or this will destroy their effectiveness. This is especially to be watched at antifouling time, if you have a willing but unknowledgeable band of helpers (personal experience!).

I think that it is fair to say that even the experts in the field don't fully understand all the problems associated with electrolysis, so all potential risks should be avoided. For example, I would keep away from alongside any copper-sheathed boat. However, the well-painted boat protected by anodes should not be in danger. But a word of warning: the trend in modern steel boats is to use thinner and thinner plate to save weight and money. While there is ample strength in, say, 3mm. plate, there is little margin for corrosion, so the owner must be all the more vigilant. The plating on older boats, such as ours, even with 25 per cent local wastage, is still thicker than that on some newer boats.

Blast Cleaning

Our real problems in surface preparation have always been below the waterline. We have spent weeks scraping, wire brushing, electric sanding and painting. And none of it was worth it, because the paint just would not stick. We tried four times with different paint schemes, but all was a waste of time and paint. We finally decided to do the job properly rather than on the cheap. So we booked for a haul out and blast clean so as to apply an epoxy paint scheme. I wish I had made that decision earlier. All the hours we have put into scraping and sanding would have more than covered the cost of the haul out and blast clean. And the cost of the paint was no more than in any of the previous years.

After carefully going into the economics of the job, I had decided to employ a firm rather than to hire the gear and do the work myself. Hire of the gear, compressor and the cost of the grit together with the cost of getting it all to the slipway, would have come to about two-thirds of the price quoted by our contractors, not to mention the trouble. The difference did not seem worth it, especially as hiring contractors would save me time. However, the cost of the grit could have been avoided. A friend of ours took the sand straight off Ramsgate beach and said that this did a fine job of cleaning although it took a lot longer than grit. But this was on ferro, and sand does not produce such a good surface as grit on steel boats. Proper surface texture is important if epoxy paints are to adhere properly. The safety experts have banned sand-blasting in commercial use because of the danger of silicosis to the operators, but a one-off operation shouldn't be fatal, provided proper helmets and face masks are worn.

The surface produced by grit blasting gives a perfect key for paint, better than any amount of wire brushing or power sanding could ever achieve. Electric sanding polishes the

63 Proper helmets, gloves and breathing apparatus are
essential for grit-blasting.

metal, whereas blasting produces a surface like fine emery
paper, and the paint can really grip. But take care not to
press your bare hands on the steel as this will leave a greasy
patch. The only faulty paint we found on subsequent slipping
was exactly in the shape of a hand-print.

Three people are really needed for the grit blasting
job—one blaster, one feeder and one painter. One missing
from the team makes the job take a lot longer, and slip time is
money. If the blaster has to feed his own abrasive, it means
removing the helmet each time and this is very tedious. And
if sand is used to save costs, clogging often occurs unless
someone is on the machine all the time. The third member of
the team is needed because the blasted area needs painting
with primer as soon as possible (on our job, I was the
painter). This is necessary to ensure that the paint goes on to
a perfectly clean and dry surface; and the first coat is the one
that counts. Additionally, epoxy paint has to go on at a

minimum temperature of 10 degrees C. (50 degrees F.) and this should be ensured if the paint is put on within about half an hour of blasting, when the steel will still be warm from the impact of the abrasive. The absolute maximum time-lag before painting is four hours—after that rust can start to form, and this will seriously diminish the paint's effectiveness.

Our job took about a day a side—5 square yards an hour seems to be a good average. We organized it so that a quarter of each side was done at a time, I then splashed on paint furiously while the operator had a rest. When he started again it was on the opposite side and at the other end of the boat to the newly painted bit. This worked well, and we didn't get any dirt in the paint, although I was careful to dust off the surface before beginning. There is a type of blaster that recycles its shot, and thus keeps everywhere reasonably clean. But these are expensive and comparatively rare. And in any event shot does not produce as good a surface as grit does on steel.

It seems that the price I was quoted was very low, and certainly I was more than satisfied. So if you can't get a sensible quote and you decide to do the work yourself, some blast-clean companies hire out the gear, or it may be obtained from some of the larger plant-hire firms.

Paint Schemes

As to the paint itself, for me the modern two-part epoxies are the only answer. They adhere to steel far more strongly than conventional paints, are almost completely impervious to water, last almost indefinitely, and have a strong resistance to chipping. There is a choice between epoxide resin composition with polyurethane on top, or epoxy tar, the latter being considerably cheaper. It is arguably harder wearing too, with considerable resistance to mechanical abrasion. It smudges rather than chips. But there is a snag as you might

246

have guessed. Epoxy tar is bitumen based, as its name implies, and will bleed through overpainting with a dark stain. So your smart white coat will end up looking something like a Friesian cow. But for us, staining was no problem as we prefer black top-coat—although we acknowledge that light-coloured topsides can be advantageous in hot sun as a way of keeping the boat cool.

As a compromise to cut down costs, if you do want light topsides, one possibility is epoxy tar below the waterline, and epoxide resin and polyurethane above. But I don't like this solution, because the join will be vulnerable; and the waterline is just where you want the most protection. No, I am afraid that a 'yachty' appearance just necessitates 'yachty' prices, so epoxide resin all over is the proper answer. But plain or fancy, epoxy can give a protection that will last almost indefinitely provided it is looked after. So in the long run it will probably work out cheaper than conventional high-build paint systems. And the protection afforded will be far greater.

In England International Paints supply both systems: Epoxy Tar or Epoxide Resin Composition followed by 708 Polyurethane. However, it pays to shop around, as epoxy paints are produced for industrial and big-ship use, and these are much cheaper. We discovered that 'Protecton Epilux' 5 Pitch Epoxy Coating (from Berger Paints) would serve our purpose, although it was sold as a general protective coating for industry. 'Protecton', which is less than half the price of International Epoxy Tar, went on very easily and comparatively quickly, which was a great advantage as I was trying to bat it on between blasting sessions. And it dried almost instantaneously so that there was no risk of the rust from subsequent blasting getting stuck into tacky paint. The International epoxy tar system on the other hand does not use a thin primer so takes longer to apply and to cure. The result of our efforts seemed fine the next time we slipped, and

I have no hesitation in recommending 'Protecton'. And my decision was backed up recently by a well-known designer, who told me that he now recommends Berger paints because they are so much cheaper. Incidentally, Berger Epoxide Resins and conventional high-build paints (Little Ship brand) are also considerably cheaper than those of International.

Conventional oil-based paints should not be used with epoxies, because they react together and the conventional paint will wrinkle up and eventually detach. I would recommend epoxies all over the outside, with oil-based paints being reserved only for the inside. And here I don't think there is anything to beat International Bare Plate Primer. This really seems to give a protection that alternative versions just don't appear to achieve. Why not epoxy inside as well? I would use epoxy inside, on a new boat, but to be effective, epoxy paint really needs blast-prepared steel. It can be worse than conventional paints without this treatment. And, unless the hull is bare, blasting inside is almost impossible.

Hot Zinc Spraying

Hot zinc spraying is in my opinion the ultimate protection for a steel boat. In this process, zinc is melted by an oxy-acetylene flame, and sprayed on the plate with a special type of gun. This gives an immensely tough coating which çan be hammered and scraped with little adverse effect. The coating is itself normally protected by a layer of paint. But if the paint is chipped, the zinc prevents the usual ugly rust streaks from forming, and stops the corrosion from creeping under the surrounding paintwork. The chips can be touched in at leisure, largely for appearance's sake, as the zinc itself will last unprotected for some considerable time before wasting away.

However, perhaps the greatest advantage of all is the galvanic protection that zinc spraying offers below the waterline. Although it is sometimes argued that the zinc underwater will rapidly be depleted by electrolysis, this is really true only if there is plenty of bronze about and no paint protection. And in any event, better the zinc to waste away than the steel. If the zinc coating is damaged and bare steel is exposed, the surrounding zinc will be sacrificed first. So the steel could in fact be left unprotected underwater for some time before being in danger.

So why is zinc spraying rarely done? The reason can't be cost alone, as expensive boats seldom get the treatment either. One argument is that modern epoxies have solved the problem of corrosion anyway. While I agree that epoxies are good, any paint can be damaged, and once it is damaged, creeping rust begins, whereas zinc has self-healing properties. I think that the real reason for the infrequent use of zinc spraying is again the lack of familiarity with steel boats in the UK. And this is borne out by the fact that zinc spraying is much more common in Holland and Belgium, where they have lived with steel boats for a lot longer.

Metco Ltd are one of the leading suppliers of metal spraying equipment, and were very helpful in providing information about the process. Sprayed metal coatings can be either anodic or cathodic to the steel. Anodic metals corrode through electrolysis, whereas cathodic metals are protected. Accordingly if steel is oversprayed with a cathodic metal, damage to the coating will result in the rapid deterioration of the underlying anodic steel. Hence we can deduce that cathodic coatings are not the ones for us (although they are used for certain applications).

TABLE OF GALVANIC SERIES OF METALS

Anodic (corroded) end

Magnesium
Zinc
Aluminium
Cadmium
Steel or iron
Cast iron
Chromium-iron (active)
18/8 Chromium-nickel-iron (active) ⎫
18/8/3 Chromium-nickel-molybdenum- ⎬ Stainless steels
   iron (active) ⎭
Lead-tin solders
Lead
Tin
Nickel (active)
Inconel (active)
Brasses
Copper
Copper-nickel alloys
Monel
Silver solder
Nickel (passive)
Inconel (passive)
Chromium-iron (passive)
18/8 Chromium-nickel-iron (passive) ⎫
18/8/3 Chromium-nickel-molybdenum- ⎬ Stainless steels
   iron (passive) ⎭
Silver
Graphite
Gold
Platinum

Cathodic (protected) end

NOTE: As can be seen, there are several varieties of stainless steel, and each type can have different percentages of the alloys, giving them a different electrolytic potential. Some of the stainless steels are anodic to commonly used metals (e.g. bronze). BEWARE OF STAINLESS BELOW THE WATERLINE.

However, only a few metals are anodic to steel (see table, p. 250), and of those available, only aluminium and zinc are suitable on practical and expense grounds. Both make excellent anodic coatings, and there is very little to choose between them in terms of ease of application or expense. Mr L. J. Walters of Metco Ltd, in an article on hot zinc spraying in the magazine *Anti-Corrosion*, states 'sprayed zinc coatings are not suitable for sea-water immersion except in very specialized applications. Corrosion of zinc in both full and half tide immersion is rapid and non-uniform, and when bare steel is exposed it apparently receives no galvanic protection after the first few years.' However, this is to be read in an industrial context, and yachts should never go 'a few years' without a hull inspection, so this amount of protection should be amply long enough for us. And although aluminium had greater impermeability and insolubility, it doesn't offer as good galvanic protection as zinc. And this is important. So in spite of Mr Walters' comments, zinc would seem to be the best choice, especially if it is itself protected by overcoating.

Zinc can be left unprotected, but it is far better painted in order to reduce permeability and to prevent anodic wastage. Metco recommend an epoxy system, but one school of thought suggests that this is unnecessary as the zinc has already encapsulated the steel, so that the much cheaper oil-based paints can be used, thereby reducing the relative cost of the total job. So it may be that antifouling below the waterline and a conventional paint scheme above will be sufficient.

Well, what about the cost? There seems to be a large disparity, even discounting relative travelling times of contractors. So it would pay to shop around. There are plenty of firms to choose from, as zinc spraying is a standard industrial process. As a rough guide, the cost of spraying would be fairly similar to the cost of grit blasting. But it would seem best to hire the same firm to blast clean and to zinc spray, as a powerful compressor is needed for both jobs, and the spraying must be done immediately after the blast cleaning.

Preparation is critical. Only blast cleaning will do, and even then the work has to be done to a very high standard. (British Standard 4232/1, or the Swedish standard SA 3 are often quoted.) And only pure metal should be used (zinc of 99·9 per cent purity to British Standard 1475).

The sprayed coating cools in a few seconds and provides instant protection. However, it is important to spray the metal on thick enough so that patches are not missed, or only thinly coated. Consequently, all areas should be sprayed with at least two passes. British Standard 2569 lays down the specification for anodic coverings, but it is up to the purchaser to state the thickness required. Some boats which are advertised as having zinc sprayed protection have only been flash sprayed for cheapness. So it is important to discover just how thick the coating is. Absolute minimum for a zinc coating would be 0·003in., but 0·005 to 0·006in. would be far better.

Zinc-Rich Paints

Another system which has retained its popularity for a long time is that of zinc-enriched paints, often known as cold galvanizing. META in France treat all their boats this way, and the results are certainly impressive. *Joshua*'s sister ship, *Vega*, was hauled out at META's yard when I visited there once. She had just come back from ten years in the West Indies, and although the paint was terrible, there was not a trace of rust anywhere. I was convinced. But zinc paint is not cheap, although it compares quite favourably with other epoxies. META have perfected their version Metagrip (formerly Dox-Anode) over a long period of time now, and there are a lot of rustless boats around to recommend it. It is obtainable from META direct. There is some debate as to whether the Metagrip should be overpainted below the waterline. Bernard Moitessier left the underwater paint bare, and claimed that the bare zinc acted as good antifouling. (See Bernard Moitessier, *Cape Horn: The Logical Route*.) However, he does stress that there should be no bronze fittings below the waterline. On the other hand META overpaint after allowing the zinc to weather for a couple of weeks, and this would seem to be safer.

In Britain, Expandite Ltd, who make the well-known Galvafroid, also produce a two-part, epoxy-based Galvafroid EV, which is intended for professional use and is not to be found in shops.

However, good though they are, these epoxy-zinc paints do not give the same protection as hot zinc spraying because the paint's electrical bonding is not so good. This is understandable, because each particle of zinc is surrounded by an insulating layer of resin.

Chlorinated Rubber
Chlorinated rubber is another preparation which has its advocates. This tough, leathery substance offers substantial resistance to mechanical abrasion, and complete impermeability. The steel yacht *Jonelle* was treated with chlorinated rubber as a protection against electrolysis below the waterline, and the owner was delighted with it. The surface preparation was done purely by scraping and wire brushing, and the climatic conditions during application were not ideal. Although initially the rubber hung in curtains and did not look very impressive, apparently the whole coating shrunk on to the steel and in a short space of time looked extremely smooth. And in the process it acquired a grip on

the steel far exceeding that of paint.

Limpetite is a derivative of the same system. This product was originally designed for the ends of chemical outfall pipes, where neither galvanized nor stainless steel would cope with the scouring effect of the outfall mixed with sand. It has tremendous resistance to mechanical abrasion, is totally impervious to water and has immense grip on the steel. I don't personally know of any steel boats that have been treated with Limpetite, but it was used on the beautifully renovated wooden smack *Gladys* in order to protect her from the dreaded Teredo worm on a trip to tropical waters. And the owner was extremely pleased.

Cheap Paints

The traditional treatment, red lead, deserves a few words. Once, most steel boats were painted with it. Now it is generally not well regarded. Below the water it saponifies and gradually detaches, then washes away. Above, it takes longer to dry than gloss topcoats. So this makes the whole lot unstable.

Is there a cheap way out? I don't think there is. And we have certainly looked for one, wasting a lot of paint in the process. With proper protection from the start, a steel boat requires no more maintenance than a two- or three-year-old resinglass craft after the gel coat has aged to the point where it starts to need cosmetic attention. With the inadequate protection afforded by 'economical' paints, you will have a constant battle against ugly rust streaks and corroding plates.

If for your own good reasons, you must make do without proper preparation, and that means abrasive blasting, the only stuff that seems to stick below the waterline is good, old-fashioned black varnish. And this is so sticky it clings to anything. But it seems to need doing regularly; it cracks after a while, and antifouling isn't very happy over the top. It is at best a temporary measure, but it does work, and it is cheap if you are hard up. It works on the topsides too, but is really suitable only for work-boats as it looks terrible and can be very messy. However, conventional high-build oil paints are OK above the waterline provided you keep your paint pot handy all the time.

Maintenance

For maintenance, as well as complete painting, surface preparation is still critical and it is important to ensure that all traces of grease and rust are removed, with any loose paint that has started to flake. The angle-grinder used with a sanding disc is useful for cleaning back really nasty areas, but is a bit vicious for run of the mill maintenance. Rubber-backed sanding discs in the electric drill are ideal for producing a good clean surface with feathered edges. Coarse-grade wet and dry sand paper (grade 120) used wet, or production paper (grade 80 or less) will do equally well if electricity is not available. Ordinary sandpaper is useless as it does not last five minutes. Sanding may not remove all the rust if pitting has occurred, and it is essential to dig out all loose rust otherwise it will react with the good metal and eventually bubble away the paint. It may be necessary to chip and scrape it away with a gouging tool. Chemical solutions such as 'Jenolite' can be useful in clearing up areas of pitting, but in my experience they don't work well on any but the least affected areas. It seems best to remove all traces of such solutions before overpainting.

Stainless Steel

I have often heard the comment that stainless steel would make the perfect boatbuilding material if only it were cheap enough. However, most 'authorities' to whom I have spoken have warned me of the dangers of using stainless steel anywhere on a boat, and especially under water. So I now tend to mistrust stainless for any purpose on a boat where strength is a requirement as opposed to pure decoration.

The problem is 'shielding' corrosion—a sophisticated form of electrolysis. If a part of a piece of stainless is shielded from oxygen, while other parts are exposed, then an electrical current can be set up and electrolysis can begin. The critical factor is the amount of oxygen over the surface of the steel, and this is why one often hears that stainless has to 'breathe'. It doesn't, but one part must not be starved of oxygen while another has it freely available. This is known as 'oxygen differential', and its presence can result in the frighteningly fast deterioration of the metal. The deterioration is usually local, quite often at a crevice and seldom detectable until too late. So if you do use stainless, it would seem prudent to have it only above the waterline. Even then fittings should be located so as to avoid an area where puddles could collect. And every fitting should be attached in such a way as to avoid the tiniest crevice which could possibly trap water.

Cor-Ten

I have mentioned this type of semi-high-tensile steel as a possible answer to corrosion in Chapter 7, when discussing choice of steel-plate. Please see page 107.

Conclusion

Corrosion protection and electrolysis are immensely complicated subjects, and even the experts disagree, and give conflicting advice. Whole books have been written on corrosion (see T. Howard Rogers, *Marine Corrosion*) and there is even a magazine on the subject—*Anti-Corrosion*, mentioned earlier. I have sifted through the available advice, sorted out some of the areas of common ground, and qualified this with my own experience. But you will have to make up your own mind as to what is best for you. I would say that a zinc-sprayed boat, epoxy-painted, would have the best protection current technology can provide. However, someone will probably even disagree with that!

16

Repairs and Alterations

The ease with which repairs can be made on a steel boat must rate as one of the big advantages of the material, and it is especially an advantage for the impoverished second-hand buyer (such as me!). This ease of repair stems from the high local strength of steel; a damaged piece can be cut out and a new piece inserted with virtually no loss of strength. Conversions can readily be carried out for the same reason. None of this is the case with GRP, ferro or wood. With GRP and ferro you may never be able to regain the original strength after damage, and a damaged wooden boat will probably require a substantial rebuild.

Most of the principles that we have looked at under welding and construction apply when it comes to repairs or alterations, but a few extra ones apply as well.

Renewing Plate

Cutting out and replacing plate is in fact a very straightforward job, which can be done afloat if the damaged area/corroded area is above the waterline. For cutting, I much prefer to use the cutting disc in the grinder, as there is much less risk of plate distortion, the job is cleaner and the grinder can readily be carried as part of the ship's equipment.

Let us start with the simplest type of repair. For example, *Abraxis* had a vent on her topsides, supposedly for the air conditioning unit (no sign of that though!). The vent had to go, as it was rusty and let in water, and its decease left a hole 6in × 12in. in the side of the hull. This was easy to fill as it was virtually flat at this point. First we cut a hardboard template to the size of the hole. Then the template was used to cut a piece of $\frac{3}{16}$in. plate to size, leaving a slight gap all around for better penetration. The plate was bevelled around the edge and tacked into place. It is best to tack at intervals all around the plate before you start to weld up, or there is serious risk of distortion. If the hole is larger than a foot or so square, to prevent distortion you may need to tack bar to the new plate and to the hull as in Fig. 66.

Tack on one edge of bar only so that the bar can be knocked against the weld to break it.

Fig 66 Fitting a new plate.

Small patches, or ones with little curvature can be put on between tides, and I would probably risk cutting the necessary hole in the boat. However, it is certainly preferable to

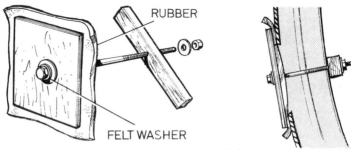

RUBBER

FELT WASHER

Fig 67 Damage control device.

haul out, so that the repair doesn't need to be rushed and can be properly painted. If the job is to be done between tides a damage control device such as in Fig. 67 would be a useful precaution (we carry these in case any of the portholes stave in). The plywood is placed over the outside of the hull and drawn up flush by tightening up the bar of wood on the inside.

Bending Plates

If the plate to be replaced is curved then some means of bending will be required. The plate-bending techniques that we looked at in Chapter 10 will be appropriate, but another version specific to repairs can also usefully be tried. The principle is best explained by the photo sequence overleaf of the tool in use on *Vic 32*. It is very simple and quick to make out of scrap steel, and it is effective and powerful, enabling $\frac{3}{16}$in. plate to be pulled around quite substantial curves. The basis of the tool is a threaded rod poked through a hole in a short piece of angle. The angle acts as a universal joint, and is securely welded to the existing hull plating adjacent to where the plate is to be bent. Next, a piece of girder section with a hole in it is slipped over the threaded rod so as to clamp up against the plate. The lazy end of the girder is packed out from the existing plating and this helps to exert tremendous pressure when the nut is tightened with the home-made wrench.

It is often useful to tack bars across the inside of the hole so that the template and then the plate can be offered up without shoving it right through! (This may be a good idea even with flat plates.) With the plate cut to the right size from the template, tack along one side of the plate so that the curvature is away from the tack as in Fig. 68. Then progressively tack on one side then the other while pulling the plate home with the appropriate bending tool. If there is excessive double curvature, straightforward

64, 65 and 66 Tool used for bending on *Vic 32*.

bending will not work as the plate will be distorted inwards
or outwards even if it can be forced home at all. Shrinkage or
cutting as discussed in Chapter 10 may work, but it is probably simpler to plate up the area of double curvature in

260

Fig 68 Plate bending.

narrow strips. These will twist to the required shape much more readily than a large plate.

Concrete Ballast

Many boats, including ours, have their ballast cemented into the bilge; this can make it harder to cut out a damaged area of plate. The only tool for this job is the grinder fitted with a cutting disc. Gas cutting will not work well as the concrete will prevent the molten metal from being blown through. The cutting disc can be made to cut out the damaged plate neatly and quickly, and will leave edges which are suitable for welding. However, the seal between cement and steel will be destroyed, and will need to be re-created in some way to prevent the plate from rusting behind. The traditional treatment is to coat the back of the plate with white lead before installation. This does not harden and will prevent the back of the plate rusting should any of the welds develop a weep. But every precaution should be taken to ensure that the welds are as perfect as possible, as they can't be double welded from the inside. This means careful preparation of the butts, so that there is an even gap and proper bevelling.

Doubling

To use a doubling plate is a doubtful practice, and many surveyors will not accept it. There are a number of reasons

261

for this. It is not possible to weld on both sides of a seam, so perfect exterior welds are necessary in order to avoid leaks. And the existing plate to which you will be welding may be suspect if doubling is required, so the strength of the welds may also be suspect. Another disadvantage is that rust can form behind the plate, and as rust expands it can eventually break the welds away. Weight will also be considerably increased by the use of doubling plates, so all in all it would seem better to avoid them.

Cutting out the old plates and accurately templating the new ones, while not difficult, will take longer than simply sticking new plate on top. But in my view such extra time is worth it, as doubling smacks of a bodged job and once you

67 An Al Mason 45 with bilge plates cut away, ready for fitting anew. The steel was eaten away paper thin because of six years of drying out every tide in a mud berth with no maintenance in that time.

start bodging on a boat it is difficult to stop. However, for replating large boats, such as ex-traders, it may be impossible to avoid doubling, as the time and expense of cutting out will probably just not be worthwhile. And doubling does mean that the job can be done between tides, thereby saving expensive slipping costs. On large boats, the extra weight of the doubling plates will probably not be significant and can usually be compensated for by removing some of the ballast. Indeed the extra ballast may even be welcome on ex-traders which seldom handle at their best unladen. Where doubling is decided upon it will be very necessary to ensure that the plate is sound where the doubler plates are to be attached. However plate usually wastes in specific areas, such as on the waterline, next to bronze underwater fittings, or under the engine. So normally it will only be these areas that require doubling and the surrounding plate will usually be sufficiently strong. In order to attach the new plate more securely to *Vic 32* Nick Walker (see Chapter 2) cut lots of small holes in the existing plate before doubling began. Then after the new plates were in position he welded old to new from the inside of the ship through these holes.

The traditional way of preventing rust behind the plate is to coat it in white lead before offering it up, and this was the technique used by a professional yard of my acquaintance during the doubling of the big iron schooner (now ketch) *Mahe*. Alternatively you can just paint bitumen on the back of the plate as was done on *Vic 32*.

Doubling on the Inside

We have in fact doubled one of *Abraxis*' plates on the inside. Aft of the rudder post, a floor without a limber hole had caused an accumulation of water which over the years had resulted in a rusty patch about 6 inches in diameter. This combined with electrolysis on the other side (near the prop) led to a leak in one spot when the scale was chipped away. I

drilled the hole out to the size of a bolt—water everywhere—and I then quickly screwed the bolt down as tight as
possible and this stopped most of the water. A little patience
enabled me to weld around the bolt and stop the leak. Ideally
the plate should have been cut out in that area and new plate
welded in, and I promised myself I would do it one day, but
for the time being I cut out $\frac{1}{8}$in. plate to fit over the rusted area
and tacked this to the plating on the inside (cutting a hole for
the bolt head). Suitable tacking and beating with a hammer
was enough to bend the $\frac{1}{8}$in. plate to the curve of the hull. I
then welded it up to the good steel surrounding the rusty
patch, making sure that the welds were as perfect as I could
make them. The next time we dried the boat out I cut the bolt
off flush to the outside of the hull, put a weld over the top and
painted. I wasn't proud of the job, but it did get me out of the
trouble, and would appear to be perfectly strong enough.

One proviso: I wouldn't advise too much welding on the
inside of the plates below the waterline without taking the
boat out of the water. The danger is that after welding the
steel will be cooled very rapidly by the outside water and can
become brittle with a risk of cracking.

It is perfectly possible to weld up leaks with water seeping
in, provided the steel is reasonably thick, although it is not
good practice. The secret is to turn the amperage higher than
normal and weld round the edge of the leak. If you are lucky
the heat will be enough to dry the seepage sufficiently for a
reasonable weld. If not, build up around the edge of the
seepage and when it is just stopped, put a broad weld over the
top.

Riveted Boats

If you have acquired a riveted boat, you will quite often find
that some of the rivets are weeping. There is a temptation to
try and weld these up from the inside, but bear in mind that
the heat off the welder will expand the steel at the join and

that you could end up chasing the leak for a long way. It is best to weld up such leaky rivets from the outside, but even then keep the heat input to a minimum and run a bead down the seam for some distance away from the rivet which is leaking, and then seal with a good quality paint, preferably an epoxy.

Iron Boats

You will sometimes come across an iron ex-trading boat, and these can represent good value. Usually of riveted construction, iron boats were not built much after the 1930s. With the popularization of mild steel, welding techniques permitted much more rapid construction than slow hand-riveting, so iron went out of favour. Iron is difficult to weld, as the area in the region of the weld can become brittle. However, I do know of two iron sailing barges that have been successfully doubled with steel plates. Ordinary rods can be used for the job, but better results will be gained with the special rods discussed in Chapter 4 (p. 62).

Iron boats do last extremely well. They are nowhere near so prone to corrosion as their modern steel counterparts and I have seen several iron barges in as good a condition as when they were first launched. If you come across one she will be well worth considering.

Under-Water Epoxy

A useful temporary repair material to carry on board is Aqua Poxy. This can be used below the waterline while still afloat, as it bonds strongly in the presence of water. It bonds to any damp surface because it dries out moisture as it cures. The brand name mentioned is obtainable in the US from Tarthang Technics. A similar product called Plastic Putty is available in England and is manufactured by Blue Peter Marine.

It is also useful to have a bag of cement on board, as this can often be used for a temporary repair while afloat. I know

265

of at least two boats (who shall be nameless) that were held afloat for the purposes of sale, purely by hardboard and cement.

17

Instrumentation

Special considerations are necessary when it comes to putting the instruments into a steel boat. The compass is the most affected, and can suffer real problems if care is not taken.

Compasses

Most big steel ships use gyro compasses, and these will be free from the magnetic interference of the hull. But they are bulky and very expensive, and so are totally out of the question for the boats in our size-range. Accordingly, magnetic compasses will have to be used.

Most steel boats have a strong magnetic pull in N–S or E–W directions, usually due to magnetism set up in the boat when building. You may well ask, what does it matter if it can be corrected, but it is not quite as simple as that for the following reasons:

1 Excessive deviation is extremely difficult to correct satisfactorily without making the compass sluggish.
2 Heeling error is the deviation which arises because the boat heels and shifts its magnetic field relative to the compass and the direction of travel. It can be split between 'permanent' error and 'soft iron' error. Permanent error can be eliminated using vertical corrector magnets but will change if the ship goes well into the hemisphere opposite to the one for which it has been adjusted. 'Soft iron' error changes with the course and latitude. It can be corrected for one latitude, but not for all.

3 Deviation in steel boats is not a static problem. It can change for a variety of reasons—lying for too long in one direction in a marina or ashore; alterations made to the steel structure; grit blasting or chipping; electric cables strung across the boat for a long time; even being on passage in the same direction for a long time; all can send ship's magnetic compasses crazy.

4 More of a problem to the voyaging steel boat is the fact that deviation changes across the world. In particular when going from the Northern Hemisphere her compasses will need to be reswung.

5 Finally, if you have an enclosed steel wheelhouse it can be difficult to persuade the magnetic compass to perform satisfactorily inside.

Deviation is an immensely complex subject, and I have only sketched over some of the main points. For a good, but lengthy exposition, see *The Complete Coastal Navigator* by Charles H. Cotter.

However, electronic magnetic repeater compasses are available, and in so far as the master compass can be sited at the null point on the boat (normally on the centre-line, roughly amidships), and it can be kept well away from her magnetic field, the effects of the magnetic field can be minimized. Accordingly the problems we have looked at will be less significant. Most systems can be made to power at least two repeater units, so one can be sighted at the inside steering positions and one outside. Perhaps the best-known make in England is 'Neco', made by Neco Marine Ltd. A slightly more expensive version is made by Cetrek Ltd.

We have a 'Neco' and it does an extremely good job. Sited 10 feet up the mast, it is out of the strongest pull of the steel hull, and before correction it gave only about 14 degrees deviation on East and West headings and virtually none when going North or South—this compared to the 45

68 'Neco' electronic magnetic repeater compass on mast of *Abraxis*.

degrees on the Danforth second compass sited down on deck. The electronic repeater is easy to read, and the movable grid makes it very easy to see the course to be maintained.

There are disadvantages, of course, and a big one is the initial expense. More important perhaps than the cost is the fact that it is risky to rely solely on a repeater because of the danger of electronic failure. Accordingly, a properly sited conventional compass must be carried. (Two compasses are a wise precaution anyway.) The electrical drain of the repeater is very slight—0·7 amps. But be careful about running the batteries right down unwittingly because that can cause the compass to give very strange readings. A more technical problem is the very slight delay between the master compass registering the course and its repetition on deck. This doesn't normally matter much except when the boat is being thrown around a lot, for example when motoring in a choppy sea left after a gale. Then the needle wanders, and it can become very difficult to steer a compass course, although this can be in part alleviated by scrupulous care in making sure that the gimbals of the master compass are moving

69 Danforth 'Corsair' magnetic compass mounted on
wood block on *Abraxis*.

freely. A quite different problem is the danger of electronic
equipment becoming rapidly outdated, with the consequent
difficulty and expense of having repairs done.

We did manage to get our Danforth 'Corsair' magnetic
compass to work entirely satisfactorily at the outside steering
position. We discovered the trick of mounting it on a solid
block of wood 6 inches high. And this substantially cut down
the deviation. It also gave somewhere to screw the corrector
magnets. It is best to mount the compass as high as you can,
so as to keep it as far as possible from the ship's magnetic
field.

As a general point when planning instrumentation,
remember that all the normal rules about the proximity of
instruments to the compass apply especially to steel boats. I
like to make sure that all radios, speakers, depth sounders,
autopilot, magnetic sensors etc. are at least 3 feet, but
preferably 6 feet, away from the compass.

Before we leave the compass, just a word about the hand-held sort. They are difficult to use on a steel boat because the deviation will change, depending whereabouts you are standing. We did some experiments and found one spot, hanging out over the stern, where deviation was down to 5 degrees in East–West heading, and nothing on North–South. (Most boats will have such a null point on the centre-line roughly amidships.) Good enough for a rough check if we make sure we stand in the right place. Better, though, is to use the hand compass not to get position lines, but to obtain position circles. If you take your bearings of terrestrial objects from the same position on the boat and you maintain a constant course, the deviation in the bearings will be constant. Accordingly, while the bearings themselves will be wrong the angles between them will be correct, and if you have three objects in the shore this will give you two position circles and you will be at their intersection. Reed's Nautical Almanac gives a full description of this method of position fixing, which I would say is essential to the steel-boat navigator. It can equally well be used with horizontal sextant angles or with the ship's compass and a pelorus.

Radio

It is difficult to persuade portable radios to work inside a steel hull. Our Hitachi just wouldn't do it. But its replacement, a National Panasonic GX.600, can usually be coaxed to perform. The National is, in fact, a remarkable radio and is the only one we have found for under £100 that will cover almost the entire short-wave band for receiving time signals world-wide (2·4–30 megacycles). It also has a direction-finding ferrite rod aerial, but that is not of much use on a steel boat. The Brookes & Gatehouse 'Homer Heron', the Electronic Laboratories Seafix and the Hitachi portable, all have this system. And none is suitable for a steel boat.

For this purpose an enclosed loop is essential and Brookes

271

70 A 'Woodson' DF loop.

& Gatehouse of Lymington recommend a very satisfactory version called the 'Woodson Loop'. It seems expensive for a comparatively simple piece of equipment, but it is easy to install. And the only other loop readily obtainable in England is the very sophisticated and even more expensive Sailor version. The 'Woodson' can incidentally be used with other than the B. & G. set. The loop will give an RDF bearing relative to the ship's head. It is comparatively difficult to use in practice, because the null and the ship's head have to be read simultaneously— not easy in a choppy sea. For this reason I do not rely on accurate position fixing with RDF but find it very useful for rough position checks and, in particular, for homing.

Accurate installation of the loop is essential, to ensure that the North point on the loop's compass card lines up with the ship's head. Any inaccuracy here will be reflected in the resulting bearing. Ideally the installation should be calibrated by taking bearings of one distant station at points relative to the boat's head equivalent to all the cardinal and intercardinal points. In this way any effect of the steel structure on the radio waves can be extracted by plotting the bearing noted at each point of the ship's head. A closed metallic loop around the boat, such as steel guard rails can have a powerful distorting effect. It should be interrupted on both sides by some insulating device.

We ourselves have the Brookes & Gatehouse Homer radio, which we use with the 'Woodson Loop'. But for ordinary medium frequency reception a separate aerial is necessary. And the correct aerial installation is essential. Many people use shrouds for this purpose. A shroud being used as an aerial has to be properly insulated from the rest of the boat, or the interference will be impossible. Brookes & Gatehouse supply special thimbles, but even with these we had trouble using a shroud, and abandoned that in favour of using thin insulated aerial wire taped to the backstay. This has produced a satisfactory performance. Even so, the receiver seems particularly susceptible to electrical interference, especially from fluorescent lights, even with the latter well insulated from the steel. It doesn't seem to be relevant how far the lights are away from the radio; so for this reason and the fact that fluorescent lights of all types appear to have a fairly limited life, we have largely gone back to filament bulbs, with paraffin as a standby.

Radio Transmitters
We find the 'Seavoice' VHF transmitter to be a most useful navigational tool, especially when cruising in strange waters. Our aerial is carried on top of the main mast, about 48 feet above the water. This gives us an incredible receiving range of over 100 miles and transmissions to shore stations of 60/70

miles. Reception is excellent and I attribute this largely to the fact that the aerial wire is very heavily insulated (UNI Radio 67) and there are no joins in the cable. The only thing that worried me is that if we lose the mast, a time when the radio may be needed to shout for help, the aerial would be out of action. For this reason I have fitted a whip aerial to the stern for use in emergency, but the latest version of Seavoice has its own aerial to meet this situation.

Many other makes are available, but the 'Seavoice' is, at the time of writing, the cheapest and is extremely reliable.

Electric Autopilots

Electric autopilots for the boats in our size range will inevitably be based on a magnetic compass, so that all the problems looked at earlier on in the chapter will also hold true here. So it is important to look for a system where the compass can be mounted remotely, out of the boat's magnetic field.

Neco Marine and Cetrek (both mentioned earlier), Marine Autopilots Ltd (Pinta), and Sharp & Co. Ltd all make suitable systems for wheel steering. My own preference would be for a 'Pinta' as I have heard nothing but favourable reports, and they certainly appear to be a robust unit. Eric Hiscock has a 'Pinta' fitted to *Wanderer IV* and praises it highly.

The compasses on autopilot are not quite so critical as the steering sort because it is only relative bearings that count. So some deviation will not matter, provided the magnetic field is not so strong as to cause a null either side of the heading sensor. This would obviously prevent course changes from registering and the autopilot would accordingly fail to work properly.

Several makes of tiller-drive autopilots are also available, but take care to choose one with a remote compass. Sharp's and Nautech Ltd. produce a suitable unit, as do Electronic

Laboratories Ltd. We have an Electronic Laboratories 'Sea-Course', modified to power our 'Hydrovane' wind steering gear.

Logs

Many types of electronic log are now available, but my own preference is for the Doppler variety of which Space Age Electronics produce an excellent and economical version.

The Doppler is ideally suited to steel as the transceiver units can be fitted to the inside of the hull plating, simply secured with plastic padding or similar. No through-hull fittings, so nothing to leak, and the installation is done in a very short time. This can only be done on steel or aluminium (or with a bit of luck GRP) as wood and ferro do not allow the sound waves to pass through (they require through-hull fittings). These units are very accurate once calibrated and the 0–8 knot speedo-scale demonstrates slight changes of speed—useful for sail trimming.

I prefer the Doppler to electromagnetic logs (such as the Electronic Laboratories version or the Brookes & Gatehouse 'Harrier') because of the risk of this type of unit exaggerating the effect of electrolysis. The Doppler works by sound waves, so does not set up electric currents within the steel hull. This advantage is in addition to the obvious one of being able to fit the unit afloat without the necessity of cutting holes in the boat.

18

Buying Second-hand
or for Home completion

Assessing a Second-hand Steel Boat

What do you look for when buying a second-hand steel boat?
When we first went to look at *Abraxis*, we hadn't a clue. We
were lucky, although we might easily not have been. So here
are a few points to watch out for, that we have discovered
subsequently. I'm not suggesting that these ideas will be a
substitute for a professional survey, but they might save you
survey money on unsuitable boats.

You will need to see a potential buy out of the water, with
any growth removed so as to get a good look. And the first
thing to look at will be the *anodes*. These can give a good clue
as to the diligence of the owner, and accordingly the likely
condition of the hull. Are there any anodes at all? If so, are
they wasted? There will probably be a white powdery substance on the surface of the anode, and this should be chipped
back to bright zinc. The white powder is depleted zinc which
offers no further protection.

If the anodes are gone, and if the paintwork is rough, then
the hull may be suspect. But not necessarily. Fortunately, it
is not difficult to test the strength of a steel hull. Whereas with
ferro or GRP, the strength largely depends on the skill of the
builder, with steel . . . well, the plate is either there, or it isn't.
And if it isn't, you can tell that with a hammer. I would
always go on an inspection armed with a light, round-headed
hammer, and a *marline spike*: the hammer to tap around the hull
for soft spots, and the spike to dig out pitting. Your seller
might be reluctant to let you loose with these weapons, but he
hasn't got much of a case if the paint is flaking or non-

existent. And if the paint is in good condition, with no sign of scaling underneath, then you have some assurance that the plating is sound. This is so, because wasting metal will quickly lift the paint off the hull. So if I were confronted with a well-painted hull, well protected with anodes, and if she were what I wanted, I would probably go ahead with the professional survey (subject to a few other points mentioned later).

Assuming we can get to work with our hammer, then the first areas to look at are those around the propeller and around any bronze underwater fittings where electrolysis is most likely. Listen for changes in note as you tap. A change might simply be due to the stiffening of a frame, but it might indicate a soft spot. In general a drop in note, or a soggy note could indicate a dodgy plate. But active electrolysis can also be detected visually. Look out for a rust-coloured crumbly growth on the surface after the boat has dried out. Scrape this off, and you will probably find a black crumbly surface underneath. Take the marline spike to this and dig away, until you have cleaned out the wasted steel and revealed the pit. Then check the maximum depth of the pits and compare this with the plate thickness (a useful depth check tool is the sort used for checking car tyre treads). About the maximum wastage normally reckoned acceptable is 25 per cent, but it clearly depends on the original thickness of the plate. And remember that pitting will necessitate grit blasting in order to clean up the surface sufficiently to get paint to stick. While isolated pitting can be cleaned up and painted, extensive pitting beyond 25 per cent may well necessitate repairs.

However, the need to make repairs is not necessarily a reason for rejecting an otherwise satisfactory boat; it is simply a reason for reducing the price.

The traditional way of testing plate thickness is to 'drill test'. Normally at least half a dozen holes will be drilled in the hull, with most of them at the suspect areas. After testing, the

277

holes are welded up inside and out. However, I am not keen on this system. I don't like drilling and welding unnecessarily and I was not prepared to go along with my insurance company's request to drill test *Abraxis*. And eventually they backed-down and accepted a hammer test.

Ultrasonic testing is an alternative, and this can work (not all that effectively) through paint, but not through scale. However, the latter is easy enough to remove at the point of testing. Strangely enough, our insurance company were not prepared to accept ultrasonic, although it would now seem to be general practice. So check with your insurers before you commission the job. The job itself should not be particularly expensive, although remember travelling costs if the tester has a long way to come.

So far I have dealt with the critical plates below the waterline, but you will need to take a look inside as well. The bilges are the place to concentrate on, as if water has been allowed to accumulate inside the hull, corrosion could well be occurring. Excessive scale should be watched for, and here the hammer can help us again. But remember that a substantial amount of scale is produced for a minimal loss in good steel.

Some boats have *standpipes* welded into the hull for rudder tubes, sink outlets etc. Because these pipes are difficult to protect they frequently corrode from the inside. So check them thoroughly for signs of weeping or softness, particularly around the base.

Many steel boats have concrete in the bilges. This is a perfectly acceptable practice, but beware any signs that the concrete has been put in recently. If so, it may well have been put in to hide thin plates. But even if the concrete appears original, it is still important to check around the edges and to make sure it isn't breaking away from the steel. If the concrete is breaking up then there is a chance of water getting in between concrete and hull plating, causing corrosion. If cracks are present, the only solution is to chip out all the concrete and replace after checking the condition of the plates. A big job—worse than replating.

And finally take a look on deck. If the boat has been neglected, there will probably be tell-tale rust streaks across the decks and down the topsides, though these are seldom serious: nothing that a chip and repaint won't cure. And rust streaks do make excellent bargaining factors.

In fact there are many bargains to be had in second-hand steel boats. People not in the know are put off by a few streaks, and the price tumbles. So you may well find it a lot cheaper to buy second-hand and renovate, than to build anew.

Hulls for Home Completion

Fitting out a hull can save you more than 50 per cent on the price of a finished boat. But don't be deceived by the amount of time it is likely to save. To give some idea, we took more than three years of part-time work to fit out and rig our 40-footer. A friend took over eighteen month's full-time work to fit out his 45-foot William Garden design, and that with a highly skilled shipwright for half of the time. The job can be done in less, though: for example, another friend designed, built and fitted out his 32-foot steel sloop in less than a year of weekends and evenings. However, you have got to be a fast worker, and it is difficult to avoid a rather raw look around the edges. But it depends what you want, a work of art or a boat to sail. And there is no doubt that for someone who wants the strongest possible boat in the shortest possible time, steel offers very real advantages. Take Bernard Moitessier's *Joshua*: telegraph poles for masts, homemade sails, basic steering and frugal interior, but a boat that could sail anywhere.

A steel hull can now be as cheap to buy as its equivalent size in ferro-cement, and the fitting out is much easier. Decks go on with no problems in fixing; furniture is simply and strongly made by tacking angle to the right shape and cladding with ply. And engine installation is comparatively straightforward.

You should not necessarily feel restricted to a home-built hull. English readers could well consider French and Dutch boats, but transport costs will be a consideration—although what about fitting out in the South of France or in Spain? At the time of writing, prices in certain Spanish yards are very competitive. Or if you are thinking of a Dutch or French boat, how about having the yard fit hatches, portholes, stern gear, engine and steerage? You could then bring her home through the canal system. All the Dutch yards have access to the system, which can take you to Calais. META in France are on the canals too, but allow a good three weeks for the trip.

One word of warning. It is very difficult to compare hull prices because different builders base their prices on different stages of completion. And as it is the finishing off that tends to cost the money, this can be misleading. Accordingly it is very important to check exactly what is included in the price—decks? engine bearers? rudder? steering? hatches? portholes? etc. However, most builders are prepared to finish their hulls to whatever state you want, and this can offer opportunities for saving money. For example, a basic hull without the decks and without the welds ground smooth could cost less than half the price of a completed hull. In my opinion, such an option is well worth considering. You avoid the skilled and heavy jobs of framing and plating and are left with the time-consuming but less tricky finishing jobs. That's not to say that these jobs can be approached lightly, but this method is a fine compromise between the daunting prospect of a pile of steel plates and the other extreme of a hull all ready for fitting out. The considerable saving can mean the difference between having and not having a boat.

Appendices

A

Addresses of Manufacturers and Suppliers Mentioned in Text

Berger Paints, Freshwater Rd., Dagenham, Essex (epoxy paint)

Blue Peter Marine, P.O. Box 10, Lancaster LA1 4UA (plastic putty)

Brookes & Gatehouse Ltd, Bath Road, Lymington, Hants. So4 9YP (instruments)

Cetrek Ltd, Balena Close, Creekmoor, Poole, Dorset. Tel: 0202 697373 (compass)

M. G. Duff & Partners Ltd, Chichester Yacht Basin, Birdham, Sussex (anodes)

Electronic Laboratories Ltd, Fleets Lane, Poole, Dorset (autopilots)

Expandite Ltd, Bracknell, Berks. (zinc paint)

J & C (Tools & Accessories) Ltd, Fairfield Rd, West Drayton, Mddx. Tel: West Drayton 45941 (Nibbler)

Marine Automatic Pilots Ltd, Waterloo St., Hove, Sussex (autopilots)

META, B.P. 109, 69170 Tarare, France (zinc paint)

Metco Ltd, Chobham, Woking, Surrey (metal spraying equipment)

Nautech Ltd, Airport Service Road, Portsmouth, Hants. (autopilots)

Neco Marine Ltd, Walton Rd., Eastern Rd., Cosham, Portsmouth, Hants. Tel: 07018 70988 (compass)

P. G. Steelcraft (Marine) Ltd, 8 Cornwall Rd., Twickenham, Mddx. (steel in kit form)

S.I.P (Industrial Products) Ltd, Radnor Rd., South Wigston, Leicester LE8 2XY (Monowelder)

Sharp & Co. Ltd, Richborough Hall, Ramsgate Rd., Sandwich, Kent (autopilots)

Space Age Electronics Ltd, Spalding Hall, Victoria Rd., London NW4 2BE (log)

Strand Glassfibre Ltd, Brentway Trading Estate, Brentford, Mddx. Tel: 01 568 7191 (expanded polyurethane foam)

Tarthang Technics, P.O. Box 1278, Berkeley, Cal. 94701, USA (underwater epoxy)

A. N. Wallis & Co. Ltd, Greasley St., Bulwell, Nottingham. Tel: 0602 271721 (hydraulic steering)

B

Designers

AUSTRALIAN

Bruce Roberts (Branches in UK, USA, Canada), Bruce Roberts Boat Plans (UK) Ltd., 73 High Street, Bexley, Kent

BRITISH

Robert Tucker, 58 Southbury Road, Enfield, Middx.

Alan Pape, Haye, Courtenay Close, East Looe, Cornwall

Maurice Griffiths, c/o Bruce Boat Plans (UK) Ltd., 73 High Street, Bexley, Kent

Peter Ibold, 15 Rue Seguier, 75006 Paris, France

FRENCH

Joseph Fricaud, META, Route de Lyon, B.P.109, 69170 Tarare

DUTCH

E. G. Van de Stadt and Partners B.V., Postbus 193 Wormerveer

USA

Al Mason, P.O. Box 5177, Virginia Beach, Va. 23455

Weston Farmer, 18970 Azure Rd., Wayzata, Minn. 55391

Jay Benford, P.O. Box 399, Friday Harbour, Wash. 98250

C

Bibliography, Including Books Mentioned in the Text

Arthur Beiser, *The Proper Yacht*, Adlard Coles 1978

Howard Chapelle, *Boat Building*, Allen & Unwin 1941

Charles H. Cotter, *The Complete Coastal Navigator*, Hollis & Carter 1964

L. Fougeron, *Si près du Cap Horn*, Ed. du Pen Duick, Paris 1974

Eric Hiscock, *Sou' West in 'Wanderer IV'*, Oxford University Press 1973

Gilbert Klingel and Thomas Colvin, *Boat Building With Steel*, International Marine Pub. Co. 1973

David Lewis, *Ice Bird*, Collins 1975

Ferenc Maté, *From a Bare Hull*, Westsail Corporation (275 McCormick Avenue, Costa Mesa, Calif. 92627) 1975

Bernard Moitessier, *Cape Horn: The Logical Route*, Adlard Coles 1969

Ian Nicolson, *Designer's Notebook: Ideas for Yachtsmen*, Adlard Coles 1970

Ian Nicolson, *Small Steel Craft*, Adlard Coles 1971

Bruce Roberts, *Build for Less*, Bruce Roberts (UK) Ltd. 1977

T. Howard Rogers, *Marine Corrosion*, Newnes-Butterworth 1968

Robert Tucker, *Fitting Out Ferro-cement Boats*, Adlard Coles 1977

A. Van de Wiele, *The West in My Eyes*, Rupert Hart-Davis 1955

Reeds Nautical Almanac

Anti-corrosion, Sawell Publications, 127 Stanstead Rd., London SE23 1JE

Index